THE ART AND SCIENCE OF
JUDO

THE ART AND SCIENCE OF
JUDO

A Guide to the Principles
of Grappling and Throwing

Jiichi Watanabe
and Lindy Avakian

New foreword by
Neil Ohlenkamp

TUTTLE Publishing

Tokyo | Rutland, Vermont | Singapore

Published by Tuttle Publishing, an imprint of Periplus Editions (HK) Ltd.,

www.tuttlepublishing.com

Copyright © 2022 Periplus Editions (HK) Ltd.
Color photography by Josh Koury. Pictured: Gary Goltz, 8th Dan, and Nathan Goltz, 5th Dan

Library of Congress Cataloging in Process

ISBN 978-0-8048-5223-4

Distributed by

North America, Latin America & Europe
Tuttle Publishing
364 Innovation Drive
North Clarendon, VT 05759-9436 U.S.A.
Tel: 1 (802) 773-8930
Fax: 1 (802) 773-6993
info@tuttlepublishing.com
www.tuttlepublishing.com

Japan
Tuttle Publishing
Yaekari Building 3rd Floor
5-4-12 Osaki
Shinagawa-ku
Tokyo 141-0032
Tel: (81) 3 5437-0171
Fax: (81) 3 5437-0755
sales@tuttle.co.jp
www.tuttle.co.jp

Asia Pacific
Berkeley Books Pte. Ltd.
3 Kallang Sector #04-01
Singapore 349278
Tel: (65) 67412178
Fax: (65) 67412179
inquiries@periplus.com.sg
www.tuttlepublishing.com

Printed in Malaysia   2110VP

25 24 23 22   10 9 8 7 6 5 4 3 2 1

TUTTLE PUBLISHING® is a registered trademark of Tuttle Publishing, a division of Periplus Editions (HK) Ltd.

Contents

Illustrations

Foreword

The Art and Science of Judo is an enduring contribution to the study of judo which provides the reader with the scientific basis and methodology to analyze techniques for critical factors impacting performance. Along the way, the authors share insights that make this new edition an important read for another generation of judo students.

When this book was first published as *The Secrets of Judo* in 1959 it was a groundbreaking achievement. Judo was largely unfamiliar outside of Japan, so its methods evoked an air of secrecy. This began changing in the United States in the 1950's, when military personnel stationed in Japan began returning home after being introduced to judo as a combative sport and form of self-defense.

Lindy Avakian, third degree black belt, served in the United States Air Force and studied judo in Japan during the early 1950's. In 1956, after 14 months of additional training, he completed the first foreign instruction course at the Kodokan Judo Institute. During his military service he trained United States Special Forces in self-defense. When he returned to California, he took on a leadership role in teaching and promoting judo.

Jiichi Watanabe was a noted instructor in Japan, sixth degree black belt, and one of the pioneers in the scientific study of judo. Together, these two authorities shed light on what makes judo work by investigating its scientific underpinnings.

This is not a book that deals with esoteric information. In fact, it helped strip away some of the mystery surrounding judo that was previously common outside of Japan. *The Secrets of Judo* has been renamed *The Art and Science of Judo* to better represent the role that science plays in the art of judo.

Jigoro Kano, the founder of judo, established the first scientific association focusing on medical studies in 1932. In 1948, the Kodokan Judo Institute expanded and renamed it the Association for the Scientific Studies on Judo. The Bulletin of the Association for the Scientific Studies on Judo began publication in 1958.

The Art and Science of Judo contributed to this evolving effort to utilize scientific inquiry. Today, the field of sports science has matured. All Olympic sports benefit from extensive study to achieve the best possible athletic performance. Judo is no exception.

The application of physics to the complex interaction between two human bodies is revealing. Physics is the natural science that studies the behavior of matter, and the energy and forces that move or control it. Physics is one of the most fundamental scientific disciplines, and its main contribution regarding judo is to understand the mechanics of how bodies behave when applying judo techniques.

After establishing the physical science applicable to judo, the last half of this book explains how these principles apply when attempting different techniques. It describes and illustrates 16 throwing and 19 grappling techniques. The text draws on the expertise of the authors as it briefly highlights key points that are critical to the execution of each technique. For improved clarity, the photographs have been updated in this edition.

Most black belts know that there is an easy way and a hard way to advance in judo. Having taught judo in many countries, I have seen beginners everywhere try to muscle through training until exhaustion. Over time, learning proper judo technique makes it easier to defeat your opponent with a skillfully applied throw, pin, or submission.

Technique must ultimately be flexible and variable, depending on your opponent's relative size, strength, speed, movement, skill, etc. You cannot memorize the correct response to every possible situation in such a fluid environment as a judo competition or practice. The process of mastering judo begins when you can apply the principles appropriately, even in new and quickly changing conditions.

After diligent study, judo training gives us the basic tools and techniques to experience the intrinsic beauty of a well-timed, seemingly effortless, technique. Even as a beginner, the power of the natural world can be felt when you are subjected to techniques that sweep you off your feet with ease.

All interactions are governed by fundamental natural forces. Gravity brings together everything, from the grappling of judoka to the orbit of the planets. Newton's theory of universal gravitation and the related laws of motion are not simply descriptions of real world behavior, but powerful tools we can use to explore the solar system or slam an opponent on the mat.

The laws of nature are universal and ever-present. They can be a source of essential power when applied to judo. Since we are striving for effortless action, success in judo requires harmonizing with the natural world.

In the first chapter, the authors say of Jigoro Kano, "He wanted a system that would be rational and logical and would develop the potential of the student's real personality. The *do* of the word judo symbolizes this philosophy." Continuous improvement requires physical training, but also demands intellectual inquiry and self-examination. Judo students often seek an effective form of self-protection, but find that striving for self-perfection is the ultimate goal in judo.

Apply yourself to all aspects of judo by carefully considering what makes it work. It turns out that experiencing the art and beauty of judo requires a thorough understanding of the science of judo. Essential topics here include reaction time, stability, laws of motion, kinds of force, overcoming friction, gripping, and how to apply throwing and grappling techniques.

Attempts at even difficult techniques will be more fruitful if you magnify the result by utilizing these concepts. Physical principles related to action/reaction, momentum, leverage, and balance apply to judo just as they govern any physical activity. Understanding the forces at work in applying a technique will help you refine your skills, maximize your effort, and make your attacks more effective.

Conversely, you may see more clearly what action is necessary to spoil an attacker's technique and prevent it from being effective against you. By exploiting the key principles involved, you not only strengthen your own actions, you can weaken those of an opponent. For example, recognizing when an opponent accelerates in order to initiate an attack, their momentum can be avoided, blocked, or redirected into a counter throw.

Because of the technical nature of this book, there are sections that require careful study. The techniques of judo are complex and require years of practice. During these years of study, it is important to enhance your understanding by including some study of the applicable science. *The Art and Science of Judo* will get you started.

The Art and Science of Judo introduced me to basic physics, psychology, kinesiology, and mechanics. It ultimately delivered a method to evaluate the efficiency of my actions and identify areas for improvement.

At the time of its original publication, there were few English language books available on judo, and no martial arts magazines, websites, social media videos, television shows, or pay-per-view. When I started learning judo in Los Angeles in the 1960's it was still difficult to get reliable information outside of class. Fortunately, I discovered this book at my local library. Detailed and thought-provoking, it sparked a lifelong search for the key principles and specific actions that give an advantage to the judo expert.

Sometimes, as you throw a skilled opponent with ease and grace, judo techniques seem to work like magic. This kind of effortless action takes a great deal of effort to finally achieve. In the process of putting in that work, I gained an appreciation for the predictable role that gravity plays, the most effective application and direction of force, how to anticipate specific reactions, using movement and leverage to overcome friction, the power of momentum in off-balancing (*kuzushi*), and other topics covered in this book.

Explaining how to effect *kuzushi* before applying a throw, the authors say, "To apply a throw successfully, you must break your opponent's posture. To do this, you must take advantage of his long reaction time. This is done by harmonizing your motion with his."

I sometimes tell my students, "Ride the horse in the direction it is going." When engaging with a larger force you should avoid futile resistance and accept the circumstance by emptying the mind and relaxing the body. Then manage the situation by harnessing the horse.

Let your opponent provide the power and calmly take the reins. Sometimes you must give up your instinctive desire to overcome in a head to head battle of force. Judo is subtle, and requires flexibility in applying techniques. This is the very meaning of judo.

The Art and Science of Judo says, "The secret of judo is serenity of mind." I encourage you to approach this new edition of a classic text in the same way. As you take your judo education into your own hands, empty your mind and open up a new way of thinking about judo.

Neil Ohlenkamp
Author, Judo Unleashed
Santa Barbara, California

1

The Art and Science of Judo

With the rapid expansion of interest in judo throughout the world today, there has developed a need for a textbook on the art and science of this sport: a textbook to be used as a reference and guide for schools, instructors, students, and the general public. The terms jujitsu and judo are common to our knowledge, but the difference in their meaning is not too clear.

Judo is a derivative of jujitsu and is the correct term used to refer to that art in today's language. The word judo specifically explains the truer meaning of the art as it is practiced today. The *ju* part of the word means "gentleness" or "giving way" and implies a flexibility of techniques, while the *do* part means "way" and signifies the application of the *ju* principle in the execution of the techniques, not only in the physical exertions of the judoist but also in his mental attitude. The older *jitsu*, which was replaced by *do*, meant "technique" or "art."

When Dr. Jigoro Kano developed judo from its original martial art form, he wanted something more than skill in technique. He theorized that what was needed was a blend of the finer techniques of jujitsu with a form of mental training or philosophy as its driving force. *Do* or "the way" therefore came to signify the mental training that the judoist needs in order to make practical use of the judo philosophy in personal contacts, daily experiences, and career relations. In other words, judo teaches the maximum efficient use of mental and physical energy.

We can say that judo is an art because it is a method of arriving at self-realization and true self-expression. We can further say that judo is a science because it implies mastery of various laws of nature: gravity, friction, momentum, velocity, weight transmission, and unison of forces. In its most important phase, it constitutes a kind of higher logic developed through practice and the ascension of the true personality: a realization of the spiritual self in the philosophic rather than the religious sense of the word.

The study of judo without the realization of its secrets—that is, its metaphysical side—leaves one in partial mental emptiness. We must first realize that the study of true judo is symbolic of mental attitudes and behavior. The subconscious mind is where our behavior patterns are collected in a vast reservoir of our years of experience. When we are able to tap these resources we can build our personalities anew, developing positive attitudes and, in the end, mastering the purely physical. It has been said, in regard to a judo expert's level of mental development, that "the arms are an extension of the mind." Training in judo disciplines the mind through physical-symbolic exercises, bringing about a maturity of the skill of higher logic. It is the use of this skill that characterizes the mental reaction of the judoist to a given situation when it arises.

At the beginning of his training, as the judoist learns the techniques of falling, mental conditioning takes over almost simultaneously with the development of physical skill. Mental control becomes an accepted reaction by the subconscious. Then, once mastery of the techniques of falling is acquired, the judoist progresses to the acquisition of skill in the techniques of throwing and, from this, to a knowledge of the principles that govern throwing and the control of balance in his body.

The beginning judoist should realize that it is better to learn the basic techniques and principles well than to oversaturate the mind with hundreds of subsidiary techniques that cannot possibly be mastered in one lifetime. In other words, it is better for the student of judo to perfect himself in the basic techniques and principles in order to set an impression on his subconscious mind. This is the result most to be desired. Once these symbolic exercises have been impressed upon the mind, the new, positive, expert attitude to situations begins to develop. Two good judo maxims illustrate the purpose of such training: *Seiryoku zenyo* means "the maximum efficient use of physical and mental energy" and *jita kyoei,* "mutual welfare and benefit."

The true value of any art form—whether it be music, painting, flower arrangement, sculpture, or judo—is that it has the goal of discovering and developing the true potential within the artist. Combative arts are patterned to challenge the expert to the development of speed, physical superiority, and mental alertness, but in judo the mental aspect is the ultimate goal of all effort, both for novices and experts. The judoist has no time to allow himself a margin for error, especially in a situation upon which his or another person's very life depends. The secret of judo is serenity of mind. The judoist must react with a conditioned reflex to any situation. It must be an automatic response, since there is no time for thinking the situation through. It must, in fact, be a state of mind such that even an attack by an opponent of greater size, or the development of a challenging situation, does not cause the judoist to change his center of balanced defense against the challenge.

This serenity of mind is developed in proper judo practice, but the true reservoir of mental composure is built through Zen meditation. Zen is a relative form of yoga, without the difficult gymnastic feats. Through correct breathing and proper postural discipline, one creates a mental state of reserved energy. Throughout the meditation period, the Zen student concentrates on "nothingness" and accepts no opposing force of any kind. He seats himself in a kneeling-sitting position in a state of relaxation as nearly complete as possible. There seems, however, to be no serious reason for the Western judoist to adopt this practice, since the Zen effect is embodied in the exercises of judo itself: exercises that require the student to re-enact the Zen performance in its adaptation to practical techniques. During free exercise, which is similar to sparring in boxing, one learns to give way "softly" to the quick movements of an opponent. These exercises also serve to train the student in adaptation to continual change. They are called *kata,* and their purpose is to teach the principles of judo.

Self-defense in judo is only one basic aspect of this art. The nucleus must be mental control, in order that mastery of the self-defense techniques may be achieved It is important for us to realize that even though

Zen originated in a religious environment, it is a philosophy and can be applied to any of our personal beliefs.

The average person, even though he does not attain ultimate mastery of true judo, can find much enjoyment in practicing its basic phases, whether he practices them as physical or mental culture, as a sport, or as a means of training in self-defense through acquiring knowledge of how to strike an opponent's vital points. In any event, such judo practice will give him a healthier body and mind, a graceful control of body balance, and increased alertness. Judo can be practiced by both men and women, boys and girls. The guidance of an instructor is very important. The relative intensity of practice can be regulated to fit the individual's needs and tolerances. Judo is a natural art. It is neither mystical nor dangerous. On the contrary, it has great value for any person, no matter what his field of endeavor may be. Few art forms can give the individual what judo has to offer.

To further understand true judo, we must go back to the origin and the ancient practice of the art in its earliest form. Every country has given the world some form of combative art between individuals. In Japan these martial arts were the sole property of the samurai class during the feudal period. Jujitsu, fencing, archery, and combat with lances were the most prominent among these. But time brought about the adoption of more modern weapons, and the martial arts took a back seat while guns, cannons, and the like occupied the foreground. By the end of the Tokugawa period (1615-1867) the martial arts had become systematized and had produced many schools with many eminent masters who developed their own styles and techniques. It was Dr. Jigoro Kano who combined the principles of the martial arts with techniques that he himself had developed and with a mental science program, thereby producing a newer art form called judo.

It should be understood that the development of judo could not allow a separation between that art and the philosophy called Zen. Therefore, if the judoist desires to reach a high level of proficiency in his art, he must learn to put into operation the principle of mind over matter. This principle explains why a smaller man is able to handle a larger attacker with seemingly magical effect. Mastery of *ju* or "giving way" is not so simple as it sounds. It is the result of sincere effort. The device of giving way until the proper time involves the use of perfect balance, rhythm and harmony, and perception—the kinesthetic or "sixth-sense" feel—of the opponent's off-balance movements. It is this that enables the judoist to gain eventual victory. When his opponent attacks, he must harmonize his own movements with the opponent's brute force in order to gain victory. Thus his preliminary retreat is performed with the goal of ultimate victory in mind. The opponent can thus be led to any disadvantageous position at will and so brought to ultimate defeat.

An attitude of overconfidence or a burning desire to win in a judo competition only preoccupies the mind and interferes with the execution of body movements, and defeat is the usual result. Judo is not, literally speaking, a form of self-defense or attack. The application of judo principles depends upon the position and movements of the opponent, but the judoist must not place himself in a situation where an effort to defend himself against his opponent's suddenly changed position may leave him exposed to attack. Thus one can see that judo does not allow rigid, set movements. Realization of this principle trains the subconscious mind to react to everyday experiences in a flexible manner, and this ability has a very important value in human contacts.

We learn, for example, that fear in its negative form cannot be accepted. We develop natural mental composure, and this calmness can be the determining factor in a situation where our very existence is at stake. The samurai developed this state of fearlessness even to the point of not fearing death. They did not feel that life was not worth worrying about, but they knew that neither the slightest amount of preoccupation nor anything else that might cause even a small mistake could be tolerated in combat.

Soon after the end of the Tokugawa period, the Restoration period was in progress in Japan, and the old forms of hand-to-hand combat were replaced by weapons of steel. The masters of the jujitsu art were dismissed from service to their feudal lords, and many turned to public showmanship as a means of making a living. The natural result was a degradation of the art.

About this time, an eighteen-year-old student, soon to become famous among Japanese educators, began his practice of jujitsu under the instruction of Professor Hachinosuke Fukuda, the eminent master of the Tenjin Shinyo-ryu school. The student, who was to become the founder of judo, was Jigoro Kano. After the death of Professor Fukuda, Dr. Kano trained under the new master of that school, Professor Masatomo Iso. Death soon took Professor Iso, however, and Dr. Kano transferred to the Kito-ryu school to study under Professor Tsunetoshi Iikubo.

Dr. Kano began to study jujitsu because of his respect for the prowess of his masters, but he soon began to thirst for a mental knowledge that was lacking in their teachings. He began to look for the secrets behind the superior expert control that the professors had mastered. He theorized that there would be greater value in combining the various schools and their techniques into one standard system: one that could be adopted as a physical education program for schools and would at the same time embody mental culture as well as physical skill. In addition, jujitsu could be practiced as a competitive sport if the more dangerous techniques were omitted. This mastery of mental culture could thus produce a pattern of subconscious behavior that would be useful in achieving "mutual welfare and benefit." He wanted a system that would be rational and logical and would develop the potential of the student's real personality. The *do* of the word judo symbolizes this philosophy.

In 1882 Dr. Kano formed his system and called it "judo," the word which has now superseded the term "jujitsu." He founded the Kodokan in Tokyo, the institution that was to become the mecca of judo. The name Kodokan is made up of three words: *ko*, meaning "to preach," *do*, meaning "way," and *kan*, meaning "hall."

Dr. Kano explained the new art of judo by pointing out that "gentleness means giving way until the right moment arrives"; that is, not to oppose the brute force of your opponent and thus to be defeated, but to utilize this force to your own advantage. Suppose that your opponent has a total force of ten units, while yours is equal to three. If he pushes toward you with a force of seven units and your force equals only three, it is futile for you to try to oppose his force, for it will overcome you. But if you give way and harmonize your force of three units with his attacking force of seven, you automatically acquire a force of ten units. Now you can defeat him because you can overcome his force of seven units with yours of ten. It can thus be appreciated that judo is a highly valuable science as well as an art. The following chapters will explain the principles of judo, and the knowledge obtained from them will be of great value to the student in mastering this art and science.

When you seek it, you cannot find it.
Your hand cannot reach it
Nor your mind exceed it.
When you no longer seek it,
It is always with you.

Zen proverb

2

How Can Dynamics Be
Applied to Judo?

IF WE wish to carry a heavy load somewhere, we use certain required tools or machines to economize our energy and time. For instance, if we are putting a large stone on a truck, by leaning a plane surface against the truck and making the stone roll or slide along it we can easily do the work, economizing our energy and, in the end, our time. This is taking advantage of both the law of resolution of forces and the law of friction, and if, in addition, we use a lever, we can do the work even more easily. This is taking advantage of the law of moment. We can make the stone roll or turn over to the right or left at will by taking advantage of dynamics. But how about the human body? A human body has a nervous system, so it can perceive your intention and make motions at its own will.

In competitive sports such as judo, wrestling, and boxing, the opponent does not move as you want. On the contrary, he will move in a direction inconvenient to your attack and defense. Hence it is difficult for you to throw or put him down, though you want to do so. Let us take an example. Seeing your opponent advance in a larger step than usual and about to rest his weight on the forward foot, you try to make him fall by sweeping his foot with your foot. But you will never succeed in felling him because his weight has already been put on the foot. Again, if you try to throw him by holding his waist with your arms, he will suddenly lower his waist. So you will not succeed in your objective because his resisting force becomes heavier than yours. Thus, in judo, the opponent tries to put his body in a position inconvenient to your attack and defense. Seemingly it is impossible for you to throw or put him down by taking advantage of dynamics. In fact, however, a small man can throw a larger man down like a puppy and hold him down easily. When you are thrown or held down, you will see many laws of dynamics at work, and you will know that they prevail.

What causes this? Isn't a human body different from a stone or a load? Doesn't it have a nervous system that makes it move freely? Two reasons can be given in answer. The first is that reaction time must be considered whenever your opponent makes a movement. The second is that you have the ability to make yourself harmonize with him. This enables you to take advantage of an opportunity to attack him; that is, to take advantage of his reaction time.

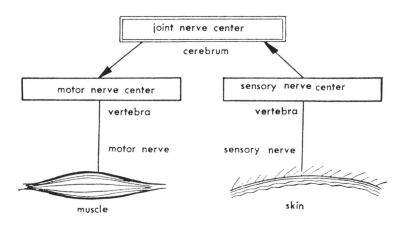

1. Nervous system: path of stimulus and response.

Nervous System

Now let us consider the nervous system. The nerves run through all parts of the body. The chief nerve centers are the brain, the spinal cord, and the sympathetic ganglia, but only the first two of these are important to the present discussion. The spinal cord runs down the spinal column. From the spinal cord a large number of nerves pass out between the vertebrae. The spinal nerves can be divided into two kinds: the sensory and the motor nerves.

1. Sensory nerves (five senses: sight, touch, taste, hearing, smell)

Why are you able to perceive your opponent's touch on your body or a change in his posture? It is because the sensory nerves running through your body are excited by external stimuli, and the resulting excitement is carried up to the sensory nerve center in the vertebrae and the joint nerve center in the cerebrum. The joint nerve center has the ability to feel excitement and remember it. By will, it can send out messages to the motor nerve center in the motor area of the cerebral cortex.

2. Motor nerves (control of muscular action: movement of fingers, working, talking, etc.)

We can make our bodies move because the muscles contract to pull the bones to which they are attached at the joints. The messages produced in the sensory area of the cerebral cortex are carried first to the motor nerve center in the motor area of the cerebral cortex, then to the vertebrae, and finally to the motor nerves running minutely through the muscles. The motor nerves there cause the proper muscles to contract. So, if the message is stopped somewhere before it reaches the end of the line, the muscles cannot contract. For instance, if the motor nerve center above the hip is broken, the leg cannot be moved at all. Again, if the motor nerves that pass through the wrist are cut off on the way, the fingers cannot move. As in the case of motor nerves, if the sensory nerve is broken, the same thing happens in the sensory area of the cerebral cortex; that is, you are shut off from everything external to the broken nerve. Now, there is an important matter with regard to the sending of stimuli and messages. This is reaction time. Let us next study this.

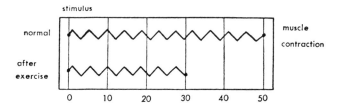

2. Reaction time.

Reaction Time

In excitation and message transfer, a time gap, like a physical solid, occurs between the stimulus and the contraction of the muscles. This time gap is called reaction time.

1. Reaction quickened by exercise

It is not known how stimuli are accepted by the joint nerve center, changed into messages, and carried to the motor nerve center, but it is clear that the time needed to produce the messages and carry them to the motor area of the cerebral cortex takes up most of the reaction time. If the same stimulus is repeatedly given, the time required for reaction is made extremely short.

Suppose a man who has never ridden a bicycle tries to ride one. At first he will probably not be able to operate it because his motor nerves do not know how to make his body balance or move when the bicycle starts to fall to the ground. Perhaps the motor nerve center has neither yet received any message from the sensory area of the cerebral cortex nor accepted the right message from it. The same thing can be said for all sports, but if the same stimulus is repeated, the joint nerve center, will act correctly and, eventually, independently of one's will. Consequently, the reaction time becomes extremely short—almost like that of an unconditioned reflex. Thus one learns by constant practice to ride a bicycle.

2. Unconditioned reflex action

If you prick your hand with a needle, you instantly pull back your hand reflexively. A bucket of water suddenly poured on your head will make you jump up reflexively. When something suddenly gets into your eye, you blink reflexively. These reactions are called unconditioned reflex actions. In these cases the stimulus is not carried to the brain but stops on the way at a vertebra where a message is produced to be sent reflexively to the motor nerve. So the path of both message and stimulus is shorter than the one that goes through the brain.

3. Conditioned reflex action

The conditioned reflex was discovered by Dr. Pavlov, a famous Russian scientist, in an experiment with a dog. A dog salivates when he eats. If a bell is rung whenever he is given food, and if this action is repeated over a period of time, the dog eventually salivates at the sound of the bell, even though he is given no food.

There is a direct relation between the flow of saliva and the food but no relation between the flow of saliva and the sound of the bell. Thus when the sound of the bell, which has no relation to the flow of saliva, is put in relation, naturally or artificially, with the reaction of producing saliva, this reaction is called conditioned reflex action. Let us give two examples.

Schoolboys get hungry the instant they hear the school bell ring for lunch. You will pull back your right arm the instant the opponent who is trying to apply right *hane-goshi* (a technique to be explained later) pivots to the left, since you have become accustomed to this way of defending yourself from *hane-goshi* as a result of long practice. In these cases the joint nerve center is never troubled. Thus no time is allowed for the joint nerve center to judge stimuli and send messages.

It is clear that the unconditioned reflex action is the shortest of the three reactions, since the path is the shortest. Next comes the conditioned reflex action, in which no time is spent in judging the stimulus and sending a message. The slowest is the reaction that travels through the joint nerve center, but we have learned that it can be shortened almost to the time span of the first by hard practice repeated daily.

4. Evaluation of the use of these three reactions in judo

a. Unconditioned reflex action

Since this reflex action is unrelated to the joint nerve center, it tends to result unconditionally from any given stimulus. In judo or boxing, for instance, if your opponent makes a movement toward your face, you are apt to close your eyes. You must not do this. If you close your eyes you cannot see him for the moment. This momentary blindness of yours gives him a good chance to attack you. Therefore this reaction must be checked by continual training.

b. Conditioned reflex action

Since this type of reaction rarely troubles the joint nerve center and comes after long acclimatization to the same stimulus, it is similar to the unconditioned reaction. In judo this reflex may not always be useful because other stimuli may be confused in certain techniques. Your opponent may take advantage of this reflex by a feint. So your joint nerve center should, first of all, analyze the various given conditions correctly and send suitable messages to the various areas.

c. Reaction achieved by practice

If you react after judgment is made in the joint nerve center, you take all the given stimuli into consideration. Therefore, unlike the conditioned reflex, which is open to deception, reaction achieved by practice enables you to exercise correct judgment in each case. It is necessary in the study of all techniques. It is not useful in a contest unless the reaction time is shortened almost to that of an unconditioned reflex action. This can be attained by continual training over a long period of time.

In judo the third type of reaction (reaction by practice) is the best of the three, and the second type (conditioned reflex action) comes next. The first type (unconditioned reflex action) does not have much use in judo.

We have studied the three kinds of short reaction time. Let us now study some cases in which the reaction time is longer.

Nine Cases in Which Reaction Time Becomes Longer

The following are typical situations or conditions in which the time required for reaction becomes longer:

1. When one is not trained in judo.
2. When one's mind or body is fatigued.
3. When one is absent-minded.

4. When one is emotionally upset.

These cases, except the first, usually occur in daily life. Even if your opponent is not proficient in judo, he will expose these weaknesses in you.

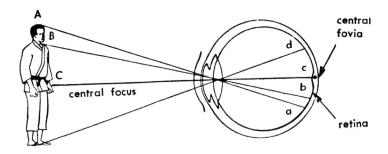

3. Object and image. Reaction time varies with clarity of image upon retina.

Next let us consider how you can lengthen the reaction time of your opponent.

5. When your opponent focuses his attention on one movement, his reaction time to another stimulus becomes long. For instance, if you try to apply *hane-goshi* in the left direction, your opponent will try to defend himself in that direction. At this moment his attention will probably be fixed in that direction only. Therefore his reaction time in the opposite direction becomes longer.

6. When stimuli are combined, the reaction time becomes longer. If your opponent knows that you can apply *hane-goshi* from both sides, he must be ready for an attack from both sides. Therefore his reaction time becomes longer.

7. When we see a movement by indirect sight, the reaction time to that movement becomes longer. When you see an object, you see some parts more clearly than the others because the central fovia of the retina can image an object clearly, but the other parts cannot. (See Figure 3.) Therefore, if you attack your opponent from a direction in which your movement cannot be clearly imaged, his reaction time becomes long.

8. When your opponent inhales, his reaction time is longer than when he exhales. We can exert a stronger force when we exhale than when we inhale. While inhaling, your opponent will find it difficult to defend himself against your attack, whether he be a master or a beginner in judo.

9. The moment your opponent is off balance in any direction, his reaction time becomes longer.

The Unguarded Moment

In addition to the foregoing nine examples of long reaction time, we must note that it takes time to move a physical solid. For example, the body or the waist and abdominal region cannot be moved as fast as the fingers or the arms. Therefore, if you are in an incorrect posture (especially standing in an unstable posture), it will take a relatively long time before you can react and take a defensive posture against your opponent's attack. It sometimes takes one-fourth to one-half a second to move into a defensive position.

What will happen if you break your opponent's posture when his long reaction time begins? He must face you unguarded. If you want to throw him, put him in such a position both physically and mentally that it takes him a longer time to get into a defensive posture; that is, break his posture. At the same time put yourself in a position, physically and mentally, in which you can attack him in as short a time as that of a reflex action. Then apply your technique. You can easily throw him. In this case you can dispose of him at will by the maximum use of dynamics.

Now let us study the cause that induces such an unguarded condition in your opponent. This factor has already been studied in the first chapter; it is that of harmonizing yourself with your opponent. To master it, you must learn the techniques of judo dynamically and physiologically and train your body to move effortlessly. In a contest, keep your mind always calm and peaceful—never get excited or panicky—so that you may systematize all the thoughts or stimuli that come into your mind into a cosmos, as an artist does when he is painting a work of art.

There will be no curtain to separate you from your opponent. You will become one with him. You and your opponent will no longer be two bodies separated physically from each other but a single entity, physically, mentally, and spiritually inseparable. Therefore the motion of your opponent may be considered your motion. And you can lure him to any posture you like and effectively apply a large force on him. You can throw him as easily as you can yourself.

3

Three Principles for Practicing Judo

IN THE previous chapter we learned about the unguarded moment: the moment that enables you to attack your opponent successfully. The unguarded moment is set up by two steps: first, by taking advantage of your opponent's long reaction time and, second, by breaking his posture before he can react. Once his posture is broken, he is certain to give you enough time to attack him successfully. In broken posture he cannot change his position and his direction of motion conveniently, and he takes a longer time to react to your attack.

Nevertheless, even a black belt judo man sometimes makes the mistake of trying to apply a throw before breaking his opponent's posture. If the opponent is also a black belt holder, he will react quickly to prevent the other man from applying a throw directly. Therefore the problem of how to break your opponent's posture is the first thing that must be studied.

Break Your Opponent's Posture before Applying Your Throw: *kuzushi* (unbalancing opponent)

It was Dr. Jigoro Kano who discovered this principle. In reporting his discovery, he said: "Mr. Iikubo was over fifty years old at the time, but he was still strong, and I used to work with him often. Although I practiced my technique industriously, I could never vie with him. I think it was about 1885 that I found, while practicing *randori* (free practice) with him, that the techniques I tried were extremely effective. Usually it had been he who threw me. Now, instead of being thrown, I was throwing him with increasing regularity. I could do this despite the fact that he was of the Kito-ryu school and was especially adept at throwing techniques.

"This apparently surprised him, and he was upset over it for quite a while. What I had done was quite unusual. But it was the result of my study of how to break the posture of the opponent. It is true that I had been studying this problem for some time, together with that of reading the opponent's motion. But it was here that I first tried to apply thoroughly the principle of breaking the opponent's posture before moving in for the throw. Afterward, at the Kodokan, I taught this principle as the *happo-no-kuzushi* (breaking the opponent's posture in eight directions) and the *roppo-no-kuzushi* (breaking the opponent's posture in six directions).

"In short, the crux of the study was that a human body would lose its balance if it was only pushed backward or pulled forward. A carelessly standing man, however large and strong, leans backward if pushed from the front and forward if pulled to the front; his posture is broken. A strong opponent, however, may be able to resist your pushing and pulling. Even so, you can easily break his posture backward if you push him backward when he pulls you forward, or pull him forward when he pushes you backward. It must be emphasized that the throw to be applied is effective only when the opponent has lost his balance.

"I told Mr. Iikubo about this, explaining that the throw should be applied after one has broken the opponent's posture. Then he said to me: 'This is right. I am afraid I have nothing more to teach you. From now on, you should continue your study with younger men. I will no longer practice with you.' And he has refrained from practicing with me since. Soon afterward, I was initiated in the mystery of the Kito-ryu jujitsu and received all his books and manuscripts of the school."

Let us study in detail how to break the opponent's posture. First we must study the stability of an object, then that of a standing human body, and finally the correct direction of breaking the posture.

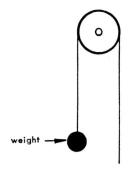

weight →

4. Gravity and weight.
   String points to center
   of earth.

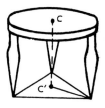

5. Center of gravity of a standing object lies on perpendicular CC' from center of
   base C'.

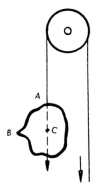

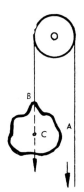

6. Center of gravity of a suspended object
   lies on line between point of attachment
   (A or B) and center of earth.

1. Stability of an object

The stability of any standing object is determined by three factors: weight, base, and position of center of gravity.

  a. Weight: The earth and every object on or near it pull toward one another. The attracting force is called gravitation. The force with which a particular object and the earth pull toward each other is called gravity. When the gravity of an object is represented by a weight unit, such as a gram, kilogram, or pound, it is called *weight*.

  b. Base: The base is a plane that supports the object.

  c. Center of gravity: If we suspend a block by a string, we see that the string points to the center of the earth. No matter where the

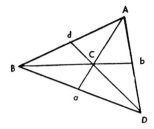

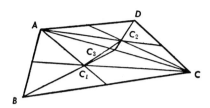

7. Finding the center of gravity in a triangle.

8. Finding the center of gravity in a trapezoid.

string is attached to the block, it is directed at a definite point on the block. This point is called the center of gravity. It is simple to find the center of gravity by experiment in the case of a block. But in a base, like a plane, it may be found geometrically. Let us now consider the plane.

Take a triangle, *ABD*. Draw three medians, *Aa, Bb,* and *Dd,* as shown in Figure 7. The three medians then intersect at one point, *C*. The point *C* is the center of gravity of the triangle *ABD*.

Figure 8 shows a trapezoid, *ABCD*. Dividing it into two triangles, *ABC* and *ACD*, find the center of gravity in each triangle: C_1 and C_2. Then find the point that divides inversely the distance between C_1 and C_2 by the ratio of magnitude of the two triangles. This point is the center of gravity of the trapezoid *ABCD*.

Figures 9 and 10 illustrate the stability and instability of standing objects. Let us tip two matchboxes to the right by taking the point *A* as an axis. If you tip the box in Figure 9 so that its center of gravity is displaced nearly to the point *E*, vertically above the axis *A*, the center of gravity will return to its original position when you let go of the box. Figure 10 shows the center of gravity just coming to the point *E*. If you keep tipping the box in the same direction, the center of gravity *C* will go down along the arc *aa'* and will not return again to its original position.

In the first case (Figure 9) we may say that the box is stable because it will return to its original position when the tipping is stopped. In the second case (Figure 10) the box is not stable because it will not return to its original position.

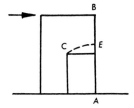

9. Center of gravity and stability of a standing object.

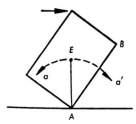

10. Center of gravity and instability of a standing object.

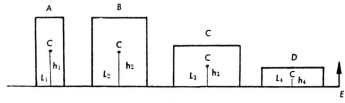

11. Relative stability of standing objects.

From the above experiments you will see that a larger force is needed to move a body when it is stable and a smaller force when it is unstable. Let us illustrate. In Figure 9 the box is stable because it takes some time to displace the center of gravity out of the base. The box in Figure 10 is unstable because it takes very little time to disturb its balance. In judo, time is needed until the posture of the opponent is made unstable. You will see that this has an important bearing on applying a throw before breaking your opponent's posture. It means that he has time to defend himself against your attack.

The stability of an object can be calculated from the ratio of the magnitude of the base to the height of the center of gravity. Let us study the following experiment:

Put four matchboxes of the same size on a plane so that they have different surfaces touching, as in A, B, C, and D in Figure 11. Let us lift the right end of plane E slowly. The boxes then start to fall one by one in the order of A, B, C, and D.

What is the reason? In the case of the boxes A and B, the height of the center of gravity is the same, but the distance between the edge and the vertical passing through the center of gravity is shorter in A (L_1 than in B (L_2). As for the boxes C and D, the reason is that the center of gravity is higher in C (h_3) than in D (h_4), though the distance between the edge and the vertical passing through the center of gravity is equal in each case. Again, in the boxes B and C, the center of gravity h_2 is higher than h_3, and the distance L_2 is shorter than the distance L_3.

2. Stability of a human body

There are many kinds of postures in judo. From among them, let us study the main natural posture, *shizen-hontai* (see Figure 13), and consider its stability. In *shizen-hontai* you stand naturally with your feet spread to a distance almost equal to the distance between your shoulders, so that the center of gravity lies at a point on the vertical line passing through the center of the base thus formed for your body.

When your right foot is put forward, the posture (Figure 12) is called *migi-shizen-tai,* or right natural posture. If the left foot is placed forward, the posture is called *hidari-shizen-tai,* or left natural posture.

Imagine a right triangle with vertices at the navel, the junction of the fourth and fifth lumbar vertebrae, and the pubis. Now find its center. This point may be taken as the position of the center of gravity when you stand in natural posture. (See Figure 14.) Let us measure the stability of the main natural posture, taking it as a rectangle. (See Figure 15.)

a. Main natural posture

Weight	75 kg
Distance between axis A and line CC' (vertical passing through center of gravity C)	12 cm
Height of center of gravity C	75 cm
Height of point of application of force F	150 cm

Assume that AB equals CC' and AD equals AC. Then, to make the body fall in the direction of the arrow F, with A as the axis, the center of gravity must be displaced from the present position C to the position D directly above point A. Therefore the work to be done is found mathematically as follows:

$$BD = AC - CC'$$
$$= \sqrt[3]{4}\overline{75^2 + 12^2} - 75$$
$$= 0.9$$
$$= 1$$

12. Right natural posture (*migi-shizen-tai*).

13. Main natural posture (*shizen-hontai*).

14. Center of gravity in main natural posture.

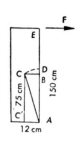

15. Stability of main natural posture.

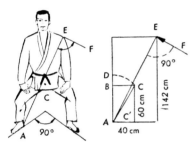

16. Main defending posture (*jigo hontai*) and its stability.

17. *Hiza-guruma* (knee wheel).
G: gravity
F: opponent's advancing force
R: resultant of F

a

b

18. *Kuzushi* (off-balancing) requires less force and time in b than in a because distance AC′ is smaller than distance A′C″.

Work = 75 kh×1 cm

= 75 kgcm

According to the theory of moment, the force F is Figured as follows:

$F \times AE$ = moment

$W \times BD$ = work

$F \times AE = W \times BD$

$$F = \frac{W \times BD}{AE}$$

$$= \frac{75}{150}$$

.5 kg (weight) or 1.2 lbs

b. *Jigo-hontai* (main defending posture)

Let us now consider *jigo-hontai,* the main defending posture. In this position, shown in Figure 16, you stand with your center of gravity low and your feet spread wider than in *shizen-hontai.* As the center of gravity is low and the base larger than in *shizen-hontai,* your body is more stable. To upset the stability of *jigo-hontai* from the side, you need a six-kilogram push.

Now let us note another instance of instability. If the center of gravity remains above a spot inside the base, the posture is called stable, but it is somewhat different when the opponent is in motion, because two forces work on him to make him fall. One of these is gravity, and the other is the force with which he moves; that is, his momentum. Let us take an instance in which the resultant passes through the axis while the center of gravity keeps its position above and within the base, as shown in Figure 17. Only a small force is needed to make your opponent fall if it acts in the same direction. Because of his own momentum, he will have difficulty changing his direction. In this case we say his posture is broken.

3. How to break the opponent's posture
a. Direction of break

In which direction should you break your opponent's posture in order to economize both time and force? As you know, the larger the base, the

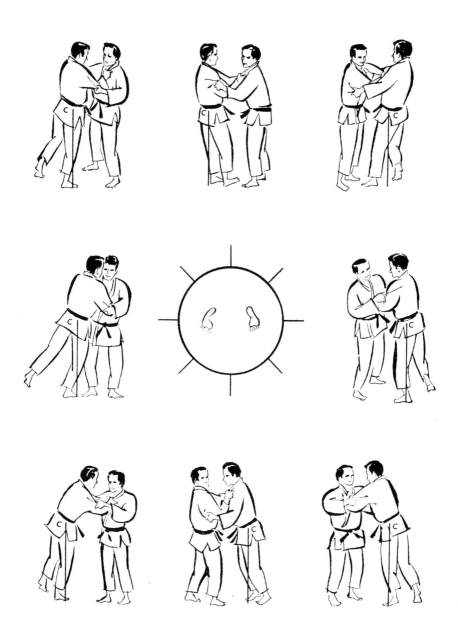

19. *Happo-no-kuzushi* (eight directions of off-balancing).

more stable a body becomes. Therefore, if your opponent stands still, it would be best for you to break his posture backwards or forwards in a direction perpendicular to the straight line passing through both his big toes. (See Figure 18.) On the other hand, if you try to break his posture toward the left or the right, the force and time needed will be increased because the base is larger.

But what happens when your opponent is in motion? In this case it is best to push or pull him in the direction of his movement. We know that a certain force works on him when he moves, together with the force that you apply. If you apply force to him in the direction in which he moves, two forces—yours and his—will work on him and cause him to lose his balance.

When he steps forward, he thinks he knows the placement of his next step. This is his mistake: his unguarded moment. Therefore, if you pull more than he pushes or push more than he pulls, his posture will be broken by the combination of forces. You must realize that if you pull or push only as much as he pushes or pulls, you cannot apply force to him.

To explain more clearly the breaking of the opponent's posture, we can classify the directions of unbalancing into the eight types called *happo-no-kuzushi*, which are illustrated in Figure 19.

b. Coordinate all parts of your body

Suppose you and your opponent stand naturally facing each other. If you pull your opponent with the power of your hands, intending to make him collapse, he will lean forward. At the same time, however, you also will lean forward. Therefore, to force him off balance without losing your own balance, you must pull him by availing yourself of the force with which you pull your own body backward and vice versa.

From the above explanation you will see that you must pull or push your opponent with your body and not with your hands only. You may then, as will be explained later, use your arm as a chain connecting your body with your opponent's, but this must be done with dexterity to apply the force of your body to him. To be exact, as Figure 85 shows, the thrower in the second diagram of *tomoe-nage* (circle throw) breaks the opponent's posture by lifting him forward with the force with which the thrower bends his body backward.

In *uki-waza* (floating throw—Figure 86) the thrower unbalances his opponent to the right front corner by taking advantage of the force (momentum) that fells the thrower backward and the force with which he twists his body from the right to the left. In *b* and *c* of *o-soto-gari* (Figure 82) too, the thrower breaks his opponent's posture backward with the force that makes his body move quickly to the opponent's right side.

It is important that you try to break your opponent's posture with your body and not with your hands only. But the body is supported by the lower extremities. It is therefore clear that the lower extremities must be used dexterously so that the body can move freely. For instance, look at the *happo-no-kuzushi* in Figure 19. You place your foot forward because you must push your body forward to break your opponent's posture backward. If you wish to break his posture forward, you must draw your foot backward. If you do not use this principle, you will pull or push with your hands only. Still, there are some cases when it is unnecessary to draw your foot backward; for example, the *tomoe-nage* and *uki-waza* techniques. In these cases, instead of drawing backward, you kick the floor with your foot to make good use of the force that is created when your body falls backward.

To be able to make good use of the lower extremities, you must realize how to use dexterously the waist and abdominal region that connects the upper body with the lower extremities. Let us, however, study this in another section, since it is very important.

Next you must realize that putting more strength in the big toes of your feet means to produce much free motion of the lower extremities. Thus, taking advantage of the coordinated working of legs, feet, waist and abdominal region, and hands, you can lure your opponent successfully to an off-balance condition in which his reaction time becomes longer.

c. Take advantage of your opponent's long reaction time

In the two sections immediately above, we have studied, first, the direction in which you can break your opponent's posture with the shortest time and force and, second, the coordination of all parts of the body for making the body work effectively. Now we must consider how to make the opponent's reaction time longer and make use of it in a practical manner.

Let us again read the section on reaction time in Chapter 2. When your opponent focuses his attention on something, his reaction time to another stimulus becomes longer. The instance of *hane-goshi* is cited in Chapter 2. We would like to take up here two other instances in which you can avail yourself of your opponent's force and his long reaction time.

It often happens that if you attack your opponent consecutively, the second or third attack enables you to make a decisive stroke. This happens because the first and second attacks put him in disorder while you are placed in a convenient position for taking advantage of his force and long reaction time. For instance, you might employ *o-uchi-gari* (see Figure 83) on him as he has leaned backward with his feet spread widely. He must push his upper body forward; otherwise, he will fall backwards. At this moment he can think of nothing but coming back into a natural posture. He doesn't realize how his pushing force is made use of by your next movement. You can now easily break his posture forward and apply *seoi-nage* (shoulder throw) or *tai-otoshi* (body drop) with success.

The second instance is that of escaping your opponent's attack. In whatever direction you advance or retreat, you must do it according to the principle of *ju*. The working of this principle will be clearly shown if you dexterously escape from his attack. He will break his posture by himself by lengthening his reaction time, since he attacks you with all his strength. At this moment your are put into a position extremely convenient for applying a throw. For example, suppose he attacks you with a right *uchi-mata* (inner thigh sweep). If you pull your left foot to the back of your right just before his body touches yours and at the same time pull his upper body with your right hand, his posture will break to his left front corner through his own force. This gives you an opportunity to apply left *tai-otoshi* (body drop) or right *ko-soto-gake* (foot hook). In case he applies left *hane-goshi* (see Figure 77) you must swerve your body aside just before he springs up your lower body with his left loin and leg and simultaneously sidestep with your left foot inside his left loin

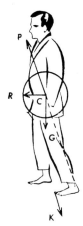

20. Dynamic coordination.
    K: force pressing ground
    P: reaction from K
    G: gravity
    R: force of advance

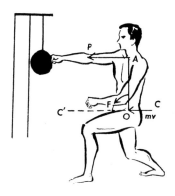

21. Coordination of forces.

while twisting your right loin backward and at the same time pulling his upper body with your left hand. He will then break toward his right front corner, giving you the best chance to hold him up with your right arm on your back waist in order to throw him down. This technique is called *utsuri-goshi* (counterattack throw).

The principle of *ju* should, as explained above, be applied only during advancing or retreating. To take advantage of both your opponent's force and his long reaction time, you must move faster and farther than he does. Through this technique, if you repeat it consecutively, you will finally bring him off balance. No matter what posture you take in accordance with his motion, you must be able to return to a position of natural posture before he attacks you. Taking this as a center that systematizes all the forces working between the two of you, you can lead him easily at your convenience, adding your force to his as you are giving way.

Take Advantage of the Waist and Abdominal Region

To apply a throw successfully, you must break your opponent's posture. To do this, you must take advantage of his long reaction time. This is done by harmonizing your motion with his. You can develop this ability through long practice. You must harmonize your motion with his, making thorough use of the forces working on you and your opponent.

You can break his posture and apply your throw with success. What is it that gives your actions vitality or life? It is the force of the waist and abdominal region, technically called the correct centripetal pressure.

How does an expert manage to move speedily, smoothly, dexterously, and lightly without losing his balance and still being able to apply a large force the moment he has broken his opponent's posture?

His own mind is always serene. It is because he can make thorough use of the force of the waist and abdominal region: correct centripetal pressure. Let us now study correct centripetal pressure.

1. The force of the waist and abdominal region coordinates all parts of the body (NOTE: This section is closely related to that on momentum in Chapter 5. Reread Chapter 3 after you have read Chapter 5.)

We can divide the human body into three parts: the lower extremities, the lower part of the trunk, and the upper body. The lower part of the trunk refers to the waist and abdominal region below the diaphragm. Located here are the major muscles supporting the spinal column, such as the musculus rectus abdominis and the oblique muscles. The major muscles that are attached to the pelvis to support the trunk are called the psoas, gluteus, quadriceps, biceps, etc.

It is important to note here that

a. The waist and abdominal region connects the upper body to the lower extremities.

b. The largest muscles of the body—and the strongest—are located here and have one end attached to the pelvis.

c. The waist and abdominal region contains about one-third of the weight of the entire body.

The waist and abdominal region, therefore, can make the muscles of the whole body coordinate dynamically. The coordination of important parts of the body could not be considered without this factor. In Figure 20, for example, the lower left extremity (hip, leg, foot) makes the whole body advance by pressing the ground. The upper body cannot comply with the will of the extremity unless the muscles of the waist and abdominal region coordinate in order to comply with the motion of the lower extremity. When these muscles comply with the

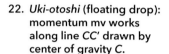

22. *Uki-otoshi* (floating drop): momentum mv works along line *CC'* drawn by center of gravity *C*.

23. Combination of forces increases speed of upward thrust.

motion of the lower extremity, all parts of the body can move in complete harmony.

In Figure 21 we have another example. Suppose you wish to punch a suspended ball with your right fist. When you advance by kicking the ground with your right leg, a momentum (see Chapter 5) is produced along the direction of the center of gravity. If, while the momentum is working, the force F, which the muscles of the lower part of the trunk exert, works to bend your body forward—that is, to rotate AO about axis O so fast that your lower body is stopped by means of reaction (see Chapter 4)—the momentum may be displaced to the upper part of the trunk, with the effect that the force P, with which your right fist punches the ball, may be represented by the displaced momentum. If you punch only with your hand, the force of the punch will be small.

Look at *o-soto-gari* in Figure 82. Letting your opponent lean backward, you (A) press the right side of your chest against his right chest by stepping with your left foot to his right side. The action of striking with your chest must be in strict accordance with that of punching the ball in Figure 21.

Next let us take up a case in which you pull your opponent forward. Look at *uki-otoshi* in Figure 22. As your opponent (B) pushes, you will draw backward, harmonizing your motion with his. The moment his body is about to lean forward, you drop your left knee to the mat suddenly, at the same time striking the mat sharply with your right foot, and pull his body down with your hands. In this case your center of gravity C draws the line $C'C''$, as seen in the Figure. The momentum produced in your body will work along the line $C'C''$. If your waist and abdominal region works so as to comply with the pull of your hands—that is, to twist your upper body strongly from right to left—the momentum will be changed into the force of your hands, which will pull him down at great speed.

From the above illustrations it is clear that whatever part of the body—hand, arm, or leg—exerts a force on an object, that force can be represented by the momentum of the whole body if the waist and the abdominal region are properly used.

Next let us take up speed. Look at Figure 23. Consider the speed with which you thrust up your fist above your head. If you do it by using your shoulder and arm alone, the distance your fist travels is only R. Now what if you also use your knees and feet? The distance your fist travels will then become P plus Q plus R, and the speed becomes much greater.

2. The force of the waist and abdominal region benefits the nervous system

We shall now explain the substance of the force of the waist and abdominal region and the relation of this force to the nervous system. Whenever one lifts a heavy object, the diaphragm contracts with the other abdominal muscles, and at the same time the loins bend backward at the junction of the fourth and fifth lumbar vertebrae, because the psoas muscle contracts, as do the other muscles attached to the pelvis. The upper body and the lower extremities now become combined into one solid mass.

When these muscles contract, pressure is produced in the abdomen. In Figure 13 we explained the position of the center of gravity when one takes a natural posture. If these muscles are contracted harmoniously, the resulting pressure works toward the center of gravity. The harmonious contraction can come only when one takes a correct posture: a posture in which the center of gravity is located just above the center of base when one is standing on both feet. The stronger the harmonious contraction, the more pressure works toward the center of gravity. The ability to unify all parts of your body into one mass, as illustrated above, is based upon the harmonious and strong contraction of the muscles of the waist and abdominal region only. Next we shall explain the relation of this pressure to the nervous system.

The late Mr. Harumitsu Hida, famous Japanese master of Zen, was one who had trained the force of the waist and abdominal region to the highest level. Mr. Kurakichi Hirata, a physiologist who received important data from Mr. Hida, studied that force scientifically. It was Mr. Hirata who named it "correct centripetal pressure." He considered it extremely important in mental training as well as in dynamic control of the whole body. Let us pick out from his famous book a few sentences pertinent to our study. He states:

"In a posture that ensures correct centripetal pressure, you can master your will more easily, promote the unified growth of the motor nerve center, and develop the nerve fibers running to the muscles from the motor center. Accordingly, the functions of the motor nerve center and the transmission of impulses from there are facilitated. Furthermore, by preserving correct centripetal pressure, the contractions, either too weak or too strong, of the chief muscles can be adjusted, while the useless contraction of antagonistic muscles is lessened, and practice can accelerate the growth of this mental and physical skill.

"Generally, the contraction of muscles becomes better coordinated. When the sensory nerve and motor nerve centers become sharper, there will be less chance to mistake impulses, and many kinds of exercises can be done more easily. In short, the ability to control the body's actions is improved."

Mr. Hirata was a pioneer in the scientific study of correct centripetal pressure. Apart from such scholastic studies, we know from daily experience that emotional disturbances, such as periods of sadness, anger, surprise, and fright, can be prevented by correct centripetal pressure.

Let us now take up the subject of respiration and its relation to centripetal pressure, for the relation is a direct one, not only to centripetal pressure but also to serenity of mind and the mastering of will

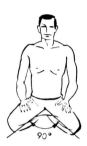

24. Right-triangle sitting position.

25. Right-triangle standing position.

power. The human body contains only about five quarts of blood. The heart circulates it from organ to organ through the blood vessels. It provides nourishment to the cells and muscles and carries waste matter from there to the lungs to be purified. If blood remains stationary in the abdomen, it is obvious that the muscles and brain will become starved and less effective in their operation. A person suffering from an upset stomach or constipation is estimated to have some one and a half quarts of impure blood in his abdomen.

If, however, the correct centripetal pressure is preserved, the stationary blood can be pushed upward toward the heart by this pressure. The heart can then do its work more easily, and the lungs can also function normally because there is less pressure from the diaphragm.

3. The force of the waist and abdominal region can be developed by training

Let us study the method of creating centripetal pressure and of invigorating the waist and abdominal region.

a. When standing or sitting, keep your body erect without bending in any direction so as to put the center of gravity just above the center of the base.

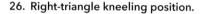

26. Right-triangle kneeling position.

27. Stepping forward in right-triangle position.

b. Project the lower part of the abdomen to the front and the hips toward the back by bending the loins at the junction of the fourth and fifth lumbar vertebrae (arching the lower back).

c. Form a right triangle with your legs when sitting (see Figure 24), with your feet when standing (see Figure 25), and with one foot and the lower half of the other leg when you have a knee on the ground (see Figure 26) in a squat-like position.

These conditions are fundamental to creating and preserving correct centripetal pressure. When you stand in the position shown in Figure 25 with your feet spread about shoulder-width, you are in natural posture, or *shizen-hontai*. Let us try a few experiments.

(1) Sit as shown in Figure 24. Next, by breaking the right angle combination, put both knees together. You will notice that the force of the waist and abdominal region becomes weaker and the body less stable. Even a slight push can knock you down. This is because the muscles of that region cannot contract vigorously and harmoniously.

Next, stand in a natural posture position. (See Figure 25.) Break the right-angle combination, pointing toes in or out. You will find that you are less stable, while the force of your waist and abdominal region becomes weaker.

Stand or sit as you wish, bending the loins forward as well as putting your center of gravity somewhere other than above the center of the base. You will find that you cannot give a strong and harmonious contraction to the muscles of the waist and abdominal region.

Advancing a step further, let us see how we can strengthen the forces of the waist and abdominal region. You can train these muscles if you sit or stand still for a long time, taking the postures described above. But the best method of training is to take advantage of the reaction produced when you step forward and drop one foot to the ground while still keeping the right-angle combination. (See Figure 27.)

Step forward with the knee bent and drop your foot quickly so that toes and heel touch the ground simultaneously. The advanced foot should make a right angle with the other foot as shown in Figure 27. At this moment you can probably shout louder (from the abdomen) than when you are standing still, and the abdominal region becomes as strong and hard as stone. This shout in judo is called *kiai* (pronounced "key-I"). The deep diaphragmatic outburst of air creates strong abdominal muscle force.

If you step out with the angle smaller than 90 degrees, the force of your step is weaker. The contraction of the muscles of the waist and abdominal region also decreases proportionately. The more vigorous the step, the stronger the correct centripetal pressure becomes. The less vigorous the step, the weaker the pressure. By taking advantage of stepping out in this manner, you can give maximum contraction to the muscles of the waist and abdominal region, with the effect that these muscles can be strengthened by training. Eventually you will be able to produce a tremendous force in the waist and abdominal region with ease. What, then, is the best posture for practicing judo?

Practice Judo in a Natural Posture

In the sections above, from the standpoints both of dynamics and the nervous system, we have learned in brief that the force of the waist and abdominal region is what controls the body's actions. A judo expert takes full advantage of this force in practice. But in throwing techniques the

28. Improper posture hampers
    use of abdominal force.

29. Defending posture
    does not permit quick
    movement.

best posture should be the one that affords a fast and light movement and at the same time permits the use of force. Let us see what this best posture is.

How about the sitting posture in Figure 24, which is similar to the basic posture in practicing Zen meditation? Although it enables you to make and preserve centripetal pressure, it is not as suitable as the natural posture shown in Figure 25. It does not permit you to move your body easily in any direction while taking advantage of your opponent's attack.

How about the posture in Figure 28, in which both arms are stretched stiffly while the loins are bent? This is abnormal, for in this posture you cannot take advantage of the power of the waist and abdominal region, nor can your movements be executed properly.

In the defending posture in Figure 29—with the feet spread more widely than in the natural posture—where is the advantage? The defending posture is better than the other two noted above, but it cannot compare with the natural posture because it is too stable. It prevents you from moving quickly in any direction. If you assume the defending posture, you may be able to change your position as fast as you can in the natural posture, but your motion will be strong and fast only in the single direction along the line passing through your feet. It can never be fast in all directions. When the center of gravity is low and the base large, the body is stable, but at the same time it is inconveniently set for a change in position and direction.

1. The natural posture is best for practicing judo

From the above illustrations it is clear that the natural posture (Figure 25) is the best position for practicing judo (in throwing techniques) because it is the most convenient for a change in position and direction. It also makes thorough use of the working power of the waist and abdominal region. If you practice judo in this posture, your waist and abdominal region will develop, and you will naturally mature both in body and in mind. Always remember that *jigo-tai* (the defensive position) is more stable than *shizen-tai* (the natural position) in a stationary situation but that, dynamically, *shizen-tai* is more stable because of its flexibility.

2. Grappling techniques require a different type of posture

In throwing, you apply techniques by taking a standing posture. But grappling is done in a prone position, or at least with one knee placed on the mat. Free and easy motions are largely limited for you as well as for your opponent. So "gentleness" or "giving way" is not so evident as it is in throwing. A lower center of gravity and a large base mean shackled motions. If your opponent is lying on the floor on his back when you attack, your motions are easier than his.

Let us consider the most effective posture for attacking your opponent in grappling. This is the posture shown in Figure 26. You place your right knee and left foot on the mat with your right foot balanced on the big toe. The left foot makes a right triangle with the lower right leg. Your center of gravity is situated directly above the center of the base.

In this position you will probably notice that you can easily push or pull an object lying in front of you without losing your balance, because your center of gravity is low and the base is large. You can also make maximum use of the waist and abdominal region. The vital work of that region is assured by the above-mentioned conditions. If you press the floor vigorously with the right knee and foot, your trunk will move forward speedily. This sets up a large momentum. How to set up and take advantage of this momentum is the secret of grappling. You may think that an expert does not attack in this manner. His varying postures should be considered as modifications as long as he tries to take advantage of the force of the waist and abdominal region.

Whenever you rest a knee on the mat, you must support the foot with the big toe bent. In this position both the leg and the foot can do their work in unison. In throwing, also, you must realize that the thorough use of the big toes is vital in making both the legs and the feet work together in one complete force.

4

Three Laws of Motion

YOU MAY have the erroneous idea that force is not necessary in judo, especially when you see a sixty-year-old instructor throwing many young and strong men seemingly without effort. Dynamics, however, denies this illusion. A body begins to move only when an external force works on it, as will be explained later. A human body is a physical entity. Therefore, if you want to break your opponent's posture and make him fall down or hold him down on the mat, you must apply the proper force to him.

In the preceding chapter we studied how to make use of the force of the waist and abdominal region to produce the largest possible force and speed. We must now study how to apply force effectively. It is properly applied force that enables you to gain victory over your opponent.

Newton's "three laws of motion" can be considered the foundation of modern dynamics. As a human body is a physical solid, its motion must be studied under these laws. Therefore a complete understanding of these laws may well be the first step toward learning the dynamics of judo. In this chapter let us create a conception of force from these laws of motion.

First Law of Motion

What is force? A conception of it can be derived from the first law of motion. Newton states that a body at rest remains eternally at rest, and a body in motion remains eternally in uniform motion unless acted upon by an external force. When we push a book that rests upon a desk or stop a ball in motion with our hands, we receive resistance from these objects.

This resistance is called inertia. Therefore, to give motion to a body at rest or to stop a body in motion, we must overcome the inertia of that body. We may define force as an action to overcome the inertia of a body.

According to the first law of motion, a rolling ball would continue eternally in motion after it had once been put in motion. Therefore, if we were to throw a ball at the moon, the ball would continue its flight until it reached the moon. In reality the ball eventually falls to earth. The reason for this is that the attraction of the earth's gravity acts on all objects in the same manner. How can we apply this law to judo? We know that if an opponent at rest makes a motion it is the result of an external force—that is, of something already independent and separated from his will—even if originally produced by his own will. Therefore you can exploit the force of your opponent if you have a good understanding of the nature of force.

For instance, assume that your opponent moves to his left with the object of making you lean to your right front corner. Suppose that the force with which he moves is equal to five units and that you can throw him in the same direction by adding a force of five units to his five. Then the total force of ten units will throw him easily, even if he tries to resist. To keep from being thrown, he must exert additional force against the force of ten units that is being placed on his body. We know that there is a force that can be exploited whenever the opponent makes a motion.

Second Law of Motion

Newton states in the second law of motion that when a force acts on a mass, the mass acquires a certain acceleration proportional to, and in the direction of, the force acting on it and that the acceleration is inverse to the magnitude of the mass. The law can be easily understood by means of the following experiment.

Suppose that there are two balls placed on the floor. One is made of iron and the other of wood. Now let us roll the balls simultaneously by applying two forces equal in magnitude and direction. The wooden ball goes farther than the iron ball because its velocity is greater. Try the experiment again, this time exerting a larger force than before. The wooden ball will roll proportionately farther and faster.

Now let us see how this law works in judo. You know that if you exert a force on your opponent and that if his body weight is less than yours, you will be able to make him move or fall with comparative ease. On the other hand, if he is heavier than you, you will have more difficulty in moving him and breaking his posture. If you throw him with a larger force, he will fall faster to the mat. If he strikes his body against yours to push you down backward, the larger his body, the more difficult it becomes for you to stop his body's movement before he applies his throw.

These phenomena are all due to the second law of motion. It is this law that shows us why a large man has an advantage over a small man in competition.

Third Law of Motion

The third law of motion is called the law of reaction. The law states that to every motion there is a reaction. We find numerous examples of this in our daily experience. If a man in a rowboat pushes another rowboat, the pushed boat moves in the direction of the force applied, while the pushing boat simultaneously makes a corresponding motion in the reverse direction. Again, if a man in a boat pushes the shore with a pole, his boat gets clear of the shore. (See Figure 30.) If a person standing in a natural posture before a pillar pushes it with his hand, he will tend to fall backward. This is due to the force of reaction that the pillar exerts against his force. (See Figure 31.)

Let us consider walking. Look at Figure 32. When a man strikes the ground backward with his lower extremity, there is produced a force of reaction, F, inverse in direction and equal in magnitude to the force K, with which he kicks. The force F is produced because the force K can kick the ground. If there is no ground to step on, there is no force F, either. It would be like trying to walk on the sea.

The reason that the man who pushes the pillar cannot exert a force greater than 0.5 kilograms without falling backward is that the pillar has strength enough to exert a reaction sufficient to overpower him. He can lift 75 kilograms from the ground because of the same fact; there is the

30. Law of reaction: force *P* produces reaction *Q*.

ground that his lower extremities can press against with the force of 75 kilograms. Therefore we find that to pull or push an object horizontally there should be a base strong enough to exert the required reaction.

Here, too, let us see what the third law of motion teaches us. Look again at Figure 31. The stability of your body can be considered as 0.5 kilograms when you stand in natural posture. Therefore, if you push the pillar with your hand, you must fall backward if your pushing force is larger than 0.5 kilograms. Nevertheless, you know that you can exert a large force horizontally on your opponent in judo practice. And the horizontal force is extremely effective in making your opponent fall.

How can you apply such a large force horizontally in spite of the third law of motion? The answer is one of the technical secrets of judo. It is that when you make your body strike against his, the force exerted on him is not only that of your hand but also that of the momentum produced in your body when it is set in motion. We shall study this momentum in Chapter 5.

The third law of motion—the law of reaction—proves that a dynamically produced force is more important than the force of the muscles in breaking the posture of the opponent and making him fall as the result of a fast and powerful movement of your body.

In grappling, why is it difficult for your opponent to get up when he is turned over on his back? It is because he has nothing to push against effectively with either of his feet. Consequently, he can use only the force of his arms and shoulders, but this is not enough to make all parts of his body cooperate.

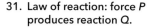

31. Law of reaction: force *P* produces reaction *Q*.

32. Kicking force *K* produces reaction force *F*. *G*: gravity.

Look at *kesa-gatame* (side collar hold) in Figure 102. A is holding B down on his back under his arm. Since A, as you can see, rests his upper body on B's chest, the pressure is considered to be the weight of A's upper body. Thus, however heavy he may be—even if he weighs 90 or 100 kilograms—B will not feel any pain because only half of A's weight is pressing him down.

When an instructor holds you down, you will feel that his body is unbelievably heavy. There are reasons for this phenomenon. One of them is that he is trying to exert the heaviest pressure possible on you. Another is the action of the third law of motion.

Look again at Figure 102. Picture yourself as A. After taking the position shown in *a*, press your chest against your opponent before you take the position shown in *b*. Then take the position shown in *b* and raise your upper body, pressing his body against your chest. To take the position shown in *b*, you raise your upper body with your chest pressed against his, at the same time continuing to hold the pressure on him. The reaction to the force with which you raise your body is produced to press heavily against his chest.

In *kesa-gatame* (side collar hold) the force that holds your opponent down results from the reaction described above, as well as from the weight of your upper body. How to apply this reaction dexterously upon your opponent is the key point of *kesa-gatame*.

5

Kinds of Force

YOU HOLD a book in your hand. If you open your hand, the book will drop to the floor immediately. The cause is the force of gravity that works on the book. When a hammer strikes the head of a nail, the nail is driven into a piece of wood. (See Figure 33.) A sled will stop when it reaches an area that is not covered with snow or ice. (See Figure 34.) Since these phenomena stem from forces that work on them, we know that there are many kinds of force around us. How are they made use of in judo? Let us now study them from this standpoint.

Muscular Force

According to Newton's second law of motion, you have an advantage over your opponent when your body is larger than his. Besides that law, however, there is another factor that gives you advantage over a smaller opponent. This is the large muscular force with which a big man is usually gifted. He can carry a heavy block or lift it easily with both hands, whereas the same feat may be difficult for a smaller man.

Although we can say that large muscular force is very convenient for breaking the opponent's posture in judo, muscular force alone does not encompass all the forces used in judo. To make use of muscular force normally and effectively, you must study its nature.

A human body is built up of about 200 bones covered and connected by 500 muscles. As Figure 35 shows, each end of a muscle is attached to a bone, with one or more joints between both ends. A muscle pulls together the two bones to which its ends are attached. Let us explain how the joints are made to bend. Look at Figure 35.

33. Force of momentum.

34. Force of friction.

One end of the biceps is attached to the upper part of the ulna. One end of the triceps is attached to the upper part of the radius. When the biceps begins to contract, the forearm begins to rotate about the elbow with the pull of the contracting biceps. If the triceps begins to contract, the forearm begins to rotate inversely about the joint. Thus the arm is straightened. It is obvious that the larger the power of the contracting biceps, the larger the weight the forearm can lift.

Let us call this power of contraction muscular force. The larger the muscle, the larger the muscular force. The force of two arms is, of course, stronger than that of one arm. A block of a certain weight that we cannot lift with one arm may be lifted easily if both arms are used. The work can be done even more easily if we do the lifting with all our muscular force by assuming the posture shown in Figure 36: with both legs bent and the center of gravity lowered.

If the body posture is not correct, and the back is not erect, and the center of gravity in the abdominal region is not stable, then the arms alone will be called upon to do the majority of work in lifting the bar bell. On the contrary, if the back is held erect and the center of gravity in the abdominal area is supported by a balanced stance, with the feet spread to about the width of the shoulders, the large muscles of the abdominal region and the legs are brought into play to support the muscles of the upper region. One of the important facts about judo is that successful employment of techniques is the result of total body muscular movement—as, for example, in the execution of an over-shoulder throw.

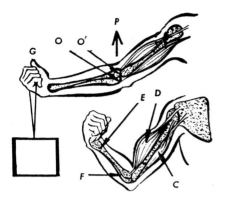

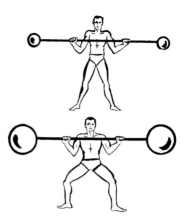

35. Muscular contraction.
   G: point of exertion   C: triceps
   O: fulcrum   D: biceps
   O': point of application E: ulna
   P: pull   F: radius

36. Partial and total
   muscular force.

The same thing can be said about making one's opponent fall or about strangling him. Defensively, too, it might be difficult to save yourself from your opponent's attack were it not for your ability to use all your muscular force. In bending your opponent's joints in reverse, the same rule applies. We can therefore understand that the exertion of a strong force means that muscles must act together by the use of the force of the waist and abdominal region.

We know that coordinated muscular force can give our bodies quick or slow, weak or strong motions at our will. This is what enables you to pull up a heavy block from the ground by making use of the force of reaction that will be produced when you kick the ground with your legs, or when you push a weight high above your head, as explained in Chapter 4. In judo you can pull your opponent's body against yours with your arms as in *hane-goshi* (spring hip throw—Figure 77) or *harai-goshi* (sweeping loin—Figure 76). In *o-uchi-gari* (major internal reaping—Figure 83) or *ko-uchi-gari* (minor internal reaping—Figure 84), you push your opponent backward to the mat with your hand. You must remember, however, that the force that pulls or pushes horizontally is not a muscular force (force of arm) as described in the passage on the third law of motion.

Let us consider the functions of the arm. If your hands pull your opponent horizontally, they serve as chains that tightly tie his body to yours. If you push him back, your arms serve as poles that cannot be bent. Besides this, there is another important work accomplished by the force of the arms. This function will be explained below in the section on momentum, which will clarify the limits of the force of the arm.

Expert judo is characterized by a large variety of techniques. As you observe, you will notice that the expert makes good use of many kinds of forces. Since judo employs many forces, such as those of gravity, momentum, and friction, you must not mistake muscular force for the only effective one. If you do, your judo will become hard, heavy, slow, and ineffective.

Gravity

In judo it is important to throw your opponent by making use of his loss of balance, as we noted in Chapter 3. One of the laws at work here is the law of gravity. We know that Sir Isaac Newton discovered the law of gravitation by seeing an apple fall from a tree. All bodies in the universe attract one another. For instance, the earth attracts the bodies near and around it. In turn they also pull the earth. Since the power of attraction, according to Newton, is proportional to the mass of the body that attracts, the larger the mass of the body, the larger its attraction. All bodies near the earth fall to the earth because it has an immense mass. An airplane or a bird starts to fall to the ground as soon as its power of flight is exhausted. The force of attraction between the earth and a two-pound weight is twice that between the earth and a one-pound weight. The attraction between the earth and a body is called gravity. When gravity is represented by weight units, it is called weight.

Now let us consider the application of the law of gravity to judo. The heavier the opponent, the more difficult it is for you to move him horizontally. It is even more difficult for you to move him vertically. On the other hand, a larger gravity acts on him to make him fall. In judo

37. Using force of gravity to assist in a throw: gravity G cooperates with force F generated by muscles pulling opponent forward.

38. Center of gravity at fulcrum; equal weight on both sides.

gravity may be represented as a force pulling the opponent downward. If you want to make him fall, you make him lose his balance; that is, you cause his center of gravity to go outside the base. Then the gravity that acts on him works for you to make him lean or fall. Let us study the action of the law of gravity by illustrations.

Look at Figure 37. You (A) and your opponent (B) are standing face to face. He advances toward you to take hold of you by the left lapel. At the same time you withdraw as much as he advances. If he is mentally or physically unable to let his advanced foot advance again, he will lean forward, lose his balance, and fall. Also, it is obvious that the same thing will happen when the stability of the legs supporting the trunk is taken away. When your opponent takes a larger step forward than usual, you merely sweep his advanced foot away in the direction of his advance, as illustrated in Figure 80 (*de-ashi-harai*, or advanced foot sweep). By doing this, you will drop him with the gravity acting on him directly.

Finally let us consider a case in which the opponent is downed by the nullification of his resistance to gravity. It may be difficult for you, because of the weight advantage of your opponent, to lift him with your arms. But it is easy to support him at the center of gravity with your loins as he leans forward. Look at the seesaw in Figure 38. A long board is supported at the center of gravity, so that the gravity on one side is equal to that on the other. Thus a slight force can rotate the board around the fulcrum. After making your opponent lean forward, support him at the center of gravity with your loins. No matter how much weight he may have, a slight pull can rotate him around your loins. To support your opponent completely at the center of gravity with your loins is the key point of such hip throws as *o-goshi*, *o-tsuri-goshi*, *ko-tsuri-goshi*, *hane-goshi*, etc. For further theoretical points of these techniques, see the discussion of moment of force in Chapter 6.

Momentum

Why is it that a little man who is proficient in judo cannot be moved even by a large man with less experience? In grappling, the smaller man

39. Momentum plus muscular force beats
    muscular force alone.

40. Momentum supplements muscular
    force in a throw. Contact of sweeping
    foot transfers force to opponent's
    ankle in *okuri-ashi-harai*.

mv

handles his opponent with the ease of a mother who cuddles her baby on her lap. Where does this wonderful force come from?

It comes from the momentum produced by a body in motion. Even now some of the secrets of the force of momentum seem hidden by a veil of ignorance. The secret is in the force of the waist and abdominal region: a force that only a great master can have at his complete control. The function of this force we have already studied in Chapter 3. Let us now look into the nature of momentum.

A blacksmith always uses a hammer when he strikes an iron bar. All of us know that the larger the striking velocity, the larger the effect upon the nail or iron bar that is struck by a hammer. Through this illustration you will see that a new force is produced in a body when it moves. This force equals the product of the weight (m) of a body and its speed (v) of motion. The product mv is called momentum. Its value is so large that everyone is surprised at seeing the product. For instance, if a body of one kilogram moves at a velocity of ten meters per second, the momentum is Figured as follows:

Momentum=mv (weight × velocity)

=1kg×10 m

= 1kg× 1,000 cm

= 1,000 kgcm per second

This Figure means that the momentum equals that of a body of 1,000 kilograms moving at a velocity of one centimeter per second. Therefore, to stop in a unit time a one-kilogram body moving at a velocity of ten meters per second, a 1,000-kilogram resistance body will be needed. And thus a little man can win over a stronger man because of his speed.

Review the above-cited Figures again. It should be clear that you, even though you may not be very large in stature, can easily throw your opponent if your attack is fast enough. Figure 40 illustrates an instance in which momentum is used to supplement muscular force. How to produce as much momentum as possible and induce it effectively in your opponent in grappling will be explained in Chapter 8. For the present let us study the law under which momentum will be induced in your opponent when you strike against him. We shall discuss this subject under four divisions: impulse, impulsive force, the application of the strongest possible force on the opponent, and the relation of momentum to the force of the arm.

1. Impulse

Drop an iron ball and try to stop it on its way down. First, stop it slowly with your hand, then stop it quickly in the shortest time possible. You will find that in the first case a comparatively small force is needed, but in the latter case a larger force is required. This is because of the law which asserts that the stopping force is proportional to the product of the mass and velocity of the body in motion and is in inverse proportion to the time required to stop that body. For instance, take the weight of the hammer, the velocity of its motion when it touches the iron bar, and the time and force required to stop it as m, v, t, and f, respectively. We then have the following equation: $ft=mv$ (force × time=weight × velocity)

We can now easily understand why we could stop a ball with a small force the first time but needed a larger force the second time. Suppose that mv (weight × velocity) is constant. Then the larger the time t, the smaller the force f. The product of the time and the force required to stop an advancing body is called impulse.

2. Impulsive force

Assume that the time required to stop a striking body is near zero. Then, from the above equation, we see that the force required to stop it will become nearly equal to the momentum. In such a case, when an attacking body is stopped in an extremely short time, the product of the force and the time is called impulsive force. We can see many examples of impulsive force every day: the striking of a ball with a bat, the blows at a boxing match, and the kicking of a foot against the ground when we jump.

3. How to apply the strongest force possible on the opponent

In judo, in order to apply a large force to your opponent, you must induce momentum in him in the shortest time possible as well as make the m (weight) express your whole weight and enlarge the v (velocity) so that mv will become greater. Let us cite an example of what makes the time t smaller in judo.

Look at *harai-goshi* in Figures 41 and 42. If you (A) sweep up the right leg of your opponent with your right leg while suddenly pulling his upper body with your hands in the direction shown by the arrow, he will be thrown down, rotating forward. In this case you turn to the left as quickly as possible by taking the posture shown in Figures 41 and 42. The momentum will be produced in your body.

41. *Harai-goshi*: less effective means of inducing momentum is to grip opponent's left lapel and right sleeve.

42. *Harai-goshi*: more effective means of inducing momentum is to place your right hand under opponent's armpit and hold his right arm between your left arm and chest.

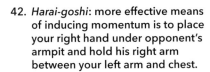

There are two ways for you to induce momentum in your opponent's upper body with your hands. (See Figure 41.) One is by gripping him by his left front lapel with your right hand and by the sleeve with your left hand. The other method (see Figure 42) is that of putting your right hand under his left armpit, at the same time holding his right arm between your left arm and the left part of your chest.

In both cases the same momentum mv will be induced in him by your hands. But the time required to stop your body will be different.

Consider which is the better of the two ways. Of course it is the latter, since in the former your opponent's lapel and sleeve serve as springs to make the time *t* longer.

4. The relation of momentum to the force of the arm

Analyze the part your arms play in judo. When the pull of your arms is weak, the time needed to induce momentum in your opponent's body will become longer. To make the time *t* shorter, a strong pull of the arms is needed. We must go a step further in studying the relation of the arm force to momentum. Since the relation may be considered the same as that between a gun and the bullet it shoots, let us approach the problem from that angle.

As the powder in the gun explodes, the bullet shoots out of the barrel, and at the same time the gun kicks back in accordance with the third law of motion. The momentums produced in the gun and the bullet are thus equal to each other. But the velocities created by the explosion of the powder are not the same because the weights of the gun and the bullet are different.

Let us take the weight and velocity of the gun as *m* and *v* and those of the bullet as $1/100\ m$ and *v'*. Then, under the third law of motion, the velocity *v'* of the bullet is as follows:

$$mv = \frac{1}{100}\ m \times v'$$

$$v' = \frac{mv \times 100}{m}$$

$$= 100v$$

Thus the bullet moves 100 times faster than the gun.

Now look at the illustration of *uki-otoshi* in Figure 22. When you drop your left knee sharply on the mat, the momentum *mv* will be produced in your body. By making use of this momentum, you pull your opponent down with both your hands. Suppose the force needed to pull him down is $1/100\ m$ weight. Then, to induce the momentum most effectively in your opponent, the velocity with which your hands pull must be 100 times faster than that with which your body moves.

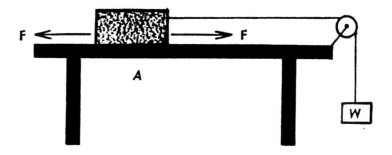

43. Friction varies with weight.

From this calculation we can see that if you push or pull your opponent with your hands, the force of the arms must induce the largest possible momentum in a certain time in your opponent.

In conclusion let us consider a few cases that make use of the large *t*. When we jump to the ground from a high place, we land on our toes first and then on our heels. We never land on our heels first. Why? Suppose your weight is 75 kilograms. Then there will be produced a large momentum until your feet touch the ground, and your feet may be injured by the impulsive force produced when they strike against the ground. But when you touch down tiptoe first, the joints of both ankles serve as springs to prevent an impulsive force. If you are thrown on the mat by your opponent, the impulsive force will injure your body unless preventive measures are taken. For this reason we are taught *ukemi* (ways of falling)—that is, how to make use of the joints of the shoulders, arms, and legs as springs—to prevent the creation of a force when the body strikes against the mat. We also use floors supported by springs and covered with mats for that purpose in our *dojo,* or places of judo practice.

Friction

If you push a heavy block on ice, it will slide freely. If a floor is oiled, we may slip and fall on it even if we walk carefully. But if the floor is rough, there is little danger of slipping. In judo we are sometimes easily made to slip on the mat. For solution of this problem we shall now study the law of friction.

Our daily experience shows us that when a block is being acted upon by a force, it will slide along a plane, but that a force that tries to prevent the block from moving is produced between the two surfaces of contact. The resisting force is usually called friction. Let us study the nature of friction. We can observe that it involves three principles.

1. The friction between two surfaces is proportional to the force pressing them together. In the apparatus shown in Figure 43 the block A has six plane surfaces, and the weight W weighs w kilograms. Suppose that W has just enough power to pull A in the direction of the pulley. Friction will be produced between the two surfaces in contact when the weight is allowed to pull the block. Let us call the friction F. Now let us place another block, B, of the same weight as A, on top of A while putting a weight W', of the same weight as W, on top of W. In this case, too, the two weights can pull the piled blocks. Thus we can see that the friction F then produced is twice the friction F formerly produced. If a third block and a third weight are added, the friction is three times as much as the first friction F. We also know that the heavier the man, the more difficult it is to make him slide or slip.

2. The friction between two surfaces depends upon the nature of their surfaces of contact. If oil is applied to the two surface of contact, we know that the friction between them becomes very small. The reason we slip easily and fall when we walk on a frosted road is that the friction between the road and our shoes is very small. In judo we are very familiar with the fact that if the mat is slippery, such foot-sweeping techniques as *de-ashi-harai* and *okuri-ashi-harai* are especially effective.

3. The friction between two surfaces is independent of the area of the surfaces of contact. An experiment will show that the friction F' produced if the block A is turned on its side will be the same as the friction F produced in the first experiment. We can therefore understand that there is no change of friction whether one stands on one foot, on both feet, or on tiptoe.

44. Friction assists in defense against a throw.

Coefficient of Friction

Since the friction (tangential force) changes proportionally to the force pressing two surfaces together (normal force), the ratio between the two forces is always constant. This ratio is usually called the coefficient of friction. Let us find the force necessary to make a man weighing 75 kilograms slide on a mat. According to experiments, the μ, or coefficient of friction between the sole of the foot and the mat is 1. If we assume μ to be equal to 1, we have the following equation:

$$\frac{F}{P} = \mu$$

$$F = \mu p$$
$$= 1 \times 75 \text{ kg}$$
$$= 75 \text{ kg} \quad \text{weight}$$

Thus we can see clearly that by using one leg alone, it is extremely difficult to make a man weighing 75 kilograms slide on a mat, since the same force as his total weight is needed to sweep that weight. So, in applying *de-ashi-harai* (advanced foot sweep), the thrower makes use of a moment when some other force will help the opponent slide.

Review *de-ashi-harai* in Figure 80. We have already studied about sweeping the opponent's advanced foot when he has taken a larger step than usual. In this case your best opportunity is to sweep his foot when he has rested almost half his total weight upon it and is about to put the other half on it. The reason for this is that the friction will be represented by the equation

$$75 \text{ kg} \times \tfrac{1}{2} = 37.5 \text{ kg}$$

and that 37.5 kilograms is less than the 75 kilograms needed to make the opponent slide and fall. Furthermore, the momentum produced when he steps forward, together with the force with which you sweep his foot, will work to overcome the friction. (Read Chapter 7, section on *de-ashi-harai*.)

Next let us study how you can defend yourself from *hane-goshi* (spring hip throw) by taking advantage of friction. Look at Figure 44. Your posture is not broken yet, but your opponent tries to apply *hane-goshi*. Friction created between the mat and the sole of your foot keeps you from rotating; your weight presses down the surfaces in contact. What prevents you from falling forward in this case is friction. Therefore, if you keep a natural posture, it is difficult for you to be thrown.

6

Acting State of Force

IN THE preceding chapter we studied the chief forces used in judo practice and arrived at a conception of force. But when we apply force to a body, many different effects are produced according to the points at which force is applied and to the direction in which it works. The same thing can be said for the number of forces to be applied. In this chapter let us study what effects are produced by a force, or forces, working under a variety of conditions. We shall learn how to apply them most effectively in judo.

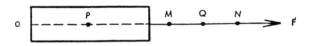

45. Transmissibility of force.

The Principle of Transmissibility of Force

In Figure 45 a string is attached to a block placed at the point P. Let us suppose that force F acts on the block by pulling the string along the line represented by the arrow. Force F acts at three places along this arrow: M, N, and O. We wish to displace the block from the point P to the point Q. We exert force F first on point M, then on point N, and finally let it push point O. Then the same effect is produced three times, and the block is displaced from point P to point Q.

By these experiments we realize that, provided the applied forces act along a single straight line and their magnitude and direction are the same, the same effect will be produced at whatever point on the straight line where they may be applied. The result is usually called the principle of the transmissibility of force. Let us observe a few applications of this principle to judo practice.

In Figure 46 the opponent (B) has leaned forward. Provided $P_1 = P_2 = P_3$ and the three forces act alike along the same line (l), the cause that makes him lean forward may be considered as the push of an external force, P_3, the force P_1, with which you (A) pull, and the force P_2, with which he advances.

Composition of Forces

The principle of *ju* is one of the most important things in judo, as we have observed in Chapter 1. It teaches us to throw the opponent by making use of his force. For instance, if you apply a force to him in the right direction, since he moves in the same direction with his own force, the force that throws him equals the sum of both forces. If you apply the force in the opposite direction to that of his force, the effective force is the result of your force minus his force. Under the principle of *ju*, to use force in that manner results in a complete waste of your energy. But if you pull him to the right front corner simultaneously as he moves to the right, in what direction is he compelled to move?

Look at Figure 47. Let us attach a string to the point O on block M. Now let us move the block by pulling the string. Let F_1 represent the pull of the string. Now let the force F_1 act on the point O. The point O will then be displaced from its present position to the point O'. Complete the parallelogram $OAO'B$ with the line OO' as the diagonal. Let OA, OO', and OB represent respectively the three forces F_1, F_2, and F_3. OA can represent the magnitude and direction of force F_2; OO', those of the force F_1; and OB, those of the force F_3. We already know that if force F_1 acts on point O, point O will be displaced from its present position to point O'. If the two forces F_2 and F_3 act on point O simultaneously, how does point O move?

Point O moves with the same velocity along the diagonal OO' to point O' and coincides with it. Therefore we can understand that the same effect will be produced whether a single force F_1 acts on point O or

46. Transmissibility of force.
    P_1: force with which you pull opponent
    P_2: force with which opponent advances
    P_3: external force

47. Parallelogram of forces.

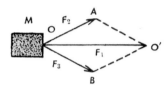

48. Composition of forces in a throw. When opponent advances with force P, you pull him down with force Q. Resultant F makes him fall forward. Line F indicates magnitude and direction of force that pulls opponent forward and down.

the two forces F_2 and F_3 act on it simultaneously, if these forces represent respectively the three lines of the parallelogram. Thus we may take the two forces F_2 and F_3, acting together, as a single force F_1.

The single force F_1 is usually called the resultant of the two forces F_2 and F_3. When the single force F_1 acts on the point O, we may consider it as the two forces F_2 and F_3 acting on it. For this reason the two forces F_2 and F_3 are called the components of the force F_1. This fact is called the principle of the parallelogram of forces. Now let us consider the application of this principle to judo.

In Figure 48a the opponent (B) is about to advance toward you (A) with the intent of grasping your lapel. In Figure 48b he has advanced his upper body by force, and you have retreated a step backwards. Now harmonize your motion with his. You pull him forward and down by force Q while force P acts on him. Then the two forces P and Q act on him together, producing a larger motion in his body. The force is the resultant F. In Figure 48c the direction and magnitude of the force that makes him bend forward is shown by the resultant (F) of the two forces P and Q.

Decomposition of Forces

When we pull a sled with a heavy load, we find that the longer the rope attached to the sled, the smaller the force needed to pull it. This is the result of the decomposition of the pulling force. Let us complete a parallelogram of force with the length of the rope as the diagonal. (See Figure 49.) Take into account that force F, which pulls the sled, works along a horizontal line. Then you will notice that the smaller the angle O, the larger the force (F_3) to pull the sled becomes. The longer the rope, the smaller the angle becomes. Let us see how this principle is made use of in grappling techniques.

To press your opponent most effectively against the mat, you must make use of the force that works vertically. Therefore it becomes important to make the vertical force larger. Look at Figure 50. The momentum will be produced when you press your chest against his. And it will work along the line of your center of gravity, CC', and resolve into two

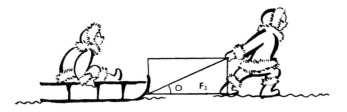

49. Decomposition of forces.

50. Modified *kami-shiho-gatame* uses larger vertical component.

51. *Kami-shiho-gatame* uses smaller vertical component.

components. So, to make the vertical force larger, you must put the center of gravity in the highest position, since the smaller the angle O', the larger the vertical component becomes. Thus we can say that modified *kami-shiho-gatame* (Figure 50) is a more effective technique than *kami-shiho-gatame* (Figure 51).

The Moment of Force

We have previously stated that different effects are produced according to the points to which force is applied. Why is this true? The reason is that a moment of force is produced whenever a force is applied at any point of a body besides the center of gravity.

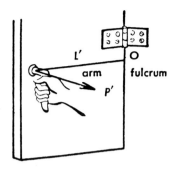

52. Moment of force operates
    to open a door.

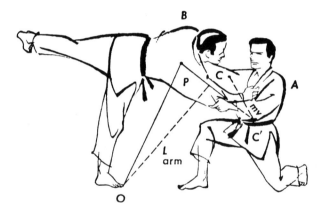

53. Arm of moment.

Look at Figures 52 and 53. The door in Figure 52 is going to open because the force *P'* acts on the handle of the door. In Figure 53 you (A) are about to throw your opponent (B) by pulling him down and forward. His right big toe serves as a fulcrum, just as the hinge of a door does.

Does the same law work in both cases? You will note that the handle of a door is placed as far as possible from the hinges, since the door can thus be opened with the minimum amount of force. In Figure 52 the

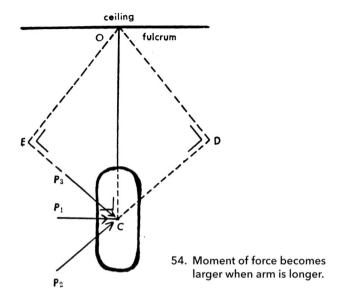

54. Moment of force becomes larger when arm is longer.

handle is placed at the distance L' from the hinge. If the handle is placed only halfway from the hinge, twice the previous force will be required.

From this experiment we find that when a force is exerted on the door, the efficiency of this force changes according to the point of application. The product of the acting force and the distance between the axis and the line of action of a force is called the moment of force. Thus the moment of force in opening the door in Figure 52 is $P'L'$, and the moment of force in rotating the opponent in Figure 53 with his right toe as a fulcrum is PL. The distance between the axis or the fulcrum and the line of action of force is called the arm. When a bar works as an arm, we call it a lever.

Let us study the arm in more detail. In Figure 54 the distance between the fulcrum and the line of action of force is a straight line drawn perpendicularly from the fulcrum to the line of force. Suppose a sandbag, C, is suspended from point O and that three forces equal in magnitude, P_1, P_2, and P_3, act on it. P_1 is acting on C perpendicularly. In the case of P_1, the arm we see is CO, because P_1 acts on it perpendicularly. In the case of P_2, the arm OD is drawn perpendicularly from the point O

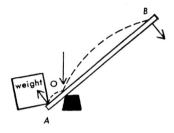

55. Arm of moment: type 1.

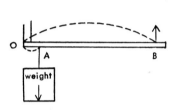

56. Arm of moment: type 2
(used in grappling).

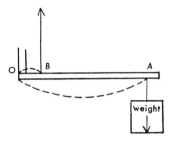

57. Arm of moment: type 3.

to the line of force P_2. In the case of P_3, the arm is *OE* for the same reason. Thus in Figure 53, if the acting force P does not act on the opponent (B) perpendicularly from the fulcrum *O*, the arm becomes *OD*, the line drawn perpendicularly from the fulcrum *O*—that is, the toes of the right foot of the opponent (B)—to the line of action of the force P. From this experiment we know that the larger the force acting on the opponent, the larger the moment of force. In the case of the arm, the moment of force becomes larger when the arm is longer.

In judo we use this principle more in grappling than in throwing. This is true because in throwing techniques we usually grasp the opponent by the sleeves, the lapel, or the upper parts of the chest. In grappling, the part of the opponent's body that should be grasped is decided by the actions of the competitors. Thus the use of the moment of force in throwing techniques is difficult to see. But in grappling, its use is very obvious. For instance, look at *kami-shiho-gatame* in Figure 51. The arm

58. Arm of moment in judo.
   A : point of exertion.
   B : point of application
   C : center of gravity
   O : fulcrum

59. Vertically applied pressure is strong; horizontally applied pressure is weak.

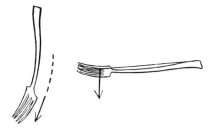

of the moment of force is short. To make it longer, you must hold your opponent down on the mat with your abdomen (see Figure 50), stretching both your legs outward in a V position.

Look at Figure 55. A straight bar is called a lever when it is used to pry up a heavy weight or a fixed object in order to take advantage of the moment of force. The fixed point O of the bar is called the fulcrum. Point A, where the bar is in contact with the force (weight) that is acted upon or resisted, is called the point of exertion. Point B, where the force is applied to the bar, is called the point of application.

Levers can be classified into three types, as shown in Figures 55, 56, and 57. The type that we use in grappling is the one that has the point of exertion A between the fulcrum O and the point of application B, as illustrated in Figure 56. Refer to the explanation of grappling techniques in Chapter 8 for further information.

What happens when you grasp your opponent by the sleeve and lapel and pull him forward? Look at Figure 58. The point of application of your pulling force is the point B on the upper part of your opponent's body. His right toes serve as a fulcrum. On the other side, the point of application of his gravity, which is opposing your pull, is the point A on the mat, vertically under the center of his gravity, C. This point is thus the point of exertion in relation to your force.

Let us now consider body movement. If you read the first part of Chapter 5 again, you will find that the human body is based and built on the principle of the moment of force. Look at Figure 35 again, keeping in mind the types of lever shown in Figures 55, 56, and 57. When you bend your elbow joint, the part to which one end of the biceps is attached becomes the point of application B; the hand represents the point of exertion A; and the elbow represents the fulcrum O. In this case the arm OB is shorter than the arm OA. Therefore, if you wish to lift a block by bending your elbow, the force that you must exert must be greater than the weight of the block. When the location of the fulcrum is changed, however, the point of exertion A will move inversely faster than the point of application B.

The construction of the human body directs it to rely on speed rather than to economize its force. Look at *okuri-ashi-harai* in Figure 81. You can sweep your opponent's foot quickly and easily. However, you must exert a strong force that comes from the waist and abdominal region, and you must make use of your opponent's weak points by twisting and bending his joints. For another example, see *juji-gatame* in Figure 119.

A jujitsu master once said: "A human body must be handled under the principle of a lever." As Figure 59 shows, if you press an object with the back of a fork held horizontally, the pressing force will be weak, but if you press vertically with the tines along the curve of the fork, the force will be stronger.

The Moment of a Couple

If you (A) and your opponent (B) are holding each other as shown in *o-soto-gari* (Figure 82), what force will you exert on him to make him

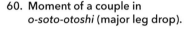

60. Moment of a couple in *o-soto-otoshi* (major leg drop).

61. Moment of a couple in *o-uchi-gari* (major inner reaping).

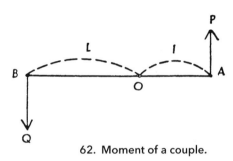

62. Moment of a couple.

fall backwards? You will probably find two ways to do this. The first way is to exert force *F* alone on the upper part of his trunk. In this case you should move fast and with controlled strength in order to prevent him from escaping by stepping back with his right foot. If he cannot do this in time, he will fall backwards. The second method is to exert two inverse forces on the upper part of his trunk and the lower extremities. There are many such instances in judo, including *o-soto-gari* (major external reaping), *o-uchi-gari* (major inner reaping), and *harai-tsurikomi-ashi* (lifting foot sweep). (See Figures 60 and 61.)

What do we mean by a couple? If the two forces *P* and *Q* are equal in magnitude and opposite in direction, the pair is called a couple. Let us study its nature.

The moment of a couple is the product of one of the forces and the distance between their lines of action. Figure 62 is an illustration of the moment of a couple. Point O is the fulcrum, and the distance between the fulcrum and the lines of action of the applied forces P and Q are L and l, respectively. Then the moment of P with respect to the fulcrum O equals Pl, and the moment of Q with respect to the fulcrum equals QL. Therefore the sum of the moments of the forces is determined as follows:

$$\text{moment} = Pl + QL$$
$$P = Q$$
$$\text{moment} = P(l + L)$$

By acting on a rigid body, a couple cannot displace it; it can only let it rotate about the fulcrum. If another external force acts on the fulcrum together with the couple, the body will move in the direction of the force, rotating about the fulcrum.

Why is a couple effective? Look at Figure 61. Since the opponent's posture has been broken to his left back corner, he will fall on his back if you push him with your right hand and reap his left leg forward (his weight rests on the heel) with the lower part of your right leg. This technique is called *o-uchi-gari*.

Why is a couple more effective in making the opponent fall on his back, as in the above-described technique, than a single force applied to the upper part of his body? The answer is that the moment a couple is applied, the opponent's left foot is reaped away from the mat, and at the same time his body drops down on the mat. But when a single force is applied on the upper part of the opponent's body, his body does not immediately drop down on the mat. It first begins to rotate toward the back with the heel as a fulcrum. Hence it takes longer to complete the throw, and the longer time gives the opponent an opportunity to defend himself from your attack.

Let us now study an instance where the application of a couple should be avoided. If you try to apply *o-soto-gari* (Figure 82) before your opponent's posture has been broken, his body will not move. The reason for this is that one part of the couple that works to reap his leg is nullified by the friction produced between his sole and the mat when you try to reap his leg from the mat. Therefore, in such a case, you must change your technique and use the reaping leg only to step behind his leg while pushing strongly against the upper part of his body.

Your pushing force can become larger, since your attacking energy is not divided into two. This technique is called *o-soto-otoshi*. However, you must make sure that pushing precedes reaping in order to throw him backward successfully. *O-soto-otoshi* is a technique based on a block-and-push type of throw that is unlike the reaping type of action in *o-soto-gari*.

7

How to Practice Throwing

Some Advice on Throwing Techniques

1. Where to hold

If you hold your opponent's right sleeve with your left hand and his left lapel with your right hand, your techniques will be limited to only the right side. If you hold him by both sleeves, you can readily apply either right or left techniques such as *hiza-guruma* or *de-ashi-harai,* but this is not true in a number of other techniques such as *hane-goshi, harai-goshi,* or *seoi-nage* (hip and hand throws). If you hold his jacket on both the right and left sides of his chest, you are well set to apply waist techniques but not *seoi-nage* (shoulder throw) or *de-ashi-harai* and *o-soto-gari,* which are foot and leg throws.

Therefore the techniques are largely restricted by the choice of where you grip and how you stand. If your opponent has enough time to defend himself from your attack, he will be able to anticipate the kind of technique you will use. You should always change the place that you grasp according to the changing positions of your opponent and yourself.

2. How to grasp

When you hold your opponent by his jacket, you should do so as gently as you would hold an egg in your hand. Always keep the forearms relaxed. If you stiffen your forearms, you are prevented not only from changing your grasp quickly but also from reading your opponent's motions. You must remember that the feel in the gripping hand is just as much an indicator of your opponent's motions as are your eyes. It is only at the moment when you apply your technique or break his posture that you must grasp tightly.

Besides these two factors there is another—perhaps the most important one. Unless your arms are kept relaxed, you cannot make good use of the force of the waist and abdominal region, which, as we have observed before, is the foundation of judo. The force of both arms is only one part of the force of the whole body; it plays its part in the harmony of the whole. Therefore, if strength is always concentrated in the arms, the over-all force of the body becomes weak.

3. How to advance or retreat

To apply throwing techniques effectively, as we have studied in the first part of Chapter 3, you must first get your opponent off-balance. This technique is called *kuzushi*. It can be used most effectively when your opponent is advancing or retreating. All you have to do is advance or retreat farther than he pulls or pushes. This is done by making use of a special way of walking called *tsugi-ashi* (special footwork), which we shall now explain.

There are two ways to walk. One is the normal way, by advancing the right and left legs alternately. In the other way of walking, a shuffle step, you first advance your right foot and then draw up the other foot until it rests about ten inches behind the right foot and is pointed outward at an angle. This is *tsugi-ashi*. In boxing too, as you know, both competitors advance or retreat in this fashion.

Which is better in judo? Of course it is *tsugi-ashi*, for it enables you to move faster than in the normal way. Furthermore, if you walk using the normal step, your posture is more vulnerable, since the time that you use to place your weight on one foot is longer than in *tsugi-ashi*.

Next you must keep in mind the correct angled-foot pattern that enables you to make the best use of the force of the waist and abdominal region. (This was studied in Chapter 3.) Then you must make the maximum use of the action of both your big toes through practice. If you can put your strength in them, you will be able to make your base larger—up to the length of the big toe. Its length amounts to one-fifth of the length of the foot. The sensory nerves running through the big toe are extremely sensitive to the loss of balance. If you take advantage of this sensitivity, your posture will be harder to break. When you put your knee on the mat, your big toe must be placed upright. This, too, will enable you to make better use of the force of the waist and abdominal region.

Ukemi: The Art of Falling

In judo the method of falling is an art in itself. Mastery of *ukemi,* or the art of falling, is essential not only for the execution of free and quick movements but also for the prevention of injury when you are thrown. Thus *ukemi* is the first technique for you to learn and master. First let us see how long it takes for a falling body to strike the mat.

When a body falling from a position at rest drops to the ground by means of gravitation, it travels 980 centimeters in the first second, 1,960 in the next second, and 2,940 in the third second. You will notice that an acceleration of 980 centimeters per second is produced uniformly every second during the fall. Since the body drops with a uniform acceleration, the average velocity is half the sum of the initial velocity and the final velocity. Average velocity can thus be expressed in the following equations, in which Vav stands for average velocity, Vo for initial velocity, Vt for final velocity, t for time, and A for acceleration:

$$1. \quad Vav = \frac{Vt+Vo}{2}$$

and since the acceleration is uniform,

$$2. \quad A = \frac{Vt-Vo}{2}$$

which results in

3. $Vt = Vo + At$

and, when Vo equals zero,

4. $Vt = At$

Now, substituting in Equation 1 the value of Vt from Equation 3:

$$5. \quad Vav = \frac{Vo+(Vo+At)}{2}$$

$$Vo = \tfrac{1}{2}At$$

63. Force in an over-shoulder throw.

Then, to find the total space S traveled in time t, we multiply the average velocity Vav by t to obtain the following:

6.　$S=Vavt$

　　$=Vot+\frac{1}{2}At^2$

By making use of Equation 6, let us find the force produced when a man weighing 75 kilograms hits the ground from a height of 1.5 meters. (See Figure 63.) If $S=\frac{1}{2}At^2$, then

1.5 m = $\frac{1}{2} \times 980$ cm/sec² $\times t^2$

$$t^2=\frac{150 \text{ cm}}{490 \text{ cm/sec}^2}$$

$$t=\frac{\sqrt[3]{415}}{7}\text{sec}^2$$

$t=0.5$ sec

Now, to find the velocity in 0.5 seconds after the man starts to fall:

$Vt=At$

　$=980$ cm $\times$ 0.5 sec

　$=490$ cm/sec

If we take the time that is required to stop the body as a unit, the resisting force of the mat is found as follows:

$mv=$resisting force of mat

　　$= 75$ kg $\times$ 490 cm/sec

　　$= 36{,}750$ kgcm/sec

64. Falling backwards from sitting, squatting, and standing positions.

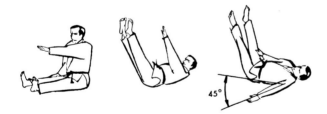

65. Falling to left side from sitting position.

66. Falling to left side from squatting position.

Now let us further study *ukemi*. Its key point is to make your upper and lower extremities strike the mat simultaneously just before your trunk makes contact. You can then utilize your shoulder, thigh, and knee joints as shock-absorbing springs to make the time t in the equation $Ft=mv$ as large as possible. If you succeed in doing so, you can break your fall by dissipating the impulsive force.

In mastering *ukemi* you first learn how to strike the mat with both your arms and hands to prevent your head from hitting it when you fall backwards. This is shown in Figure 64. The arms are straight and make an angle of about 45 degrees with the trunk. Strike the mat as vigorously as possible with both arms and hands.

Next you must learn to make one arm and hand strike the mat sideways to the left. In Figures 65 and 66 the left hand and arm strike the mat toward the left. Then you must suddenly drop them on the mat and make them strike simultaneously and as strongly as possible. Repeat the practice alternately right and left in daily workouts.

Next, as shown in Figure 67, learn to make one arm and one hand, one leg and one foot, and the sole of the other foot strike the mat simultaneously as you fall. After you have learned these ways of striking the mat, you advance further to the practice of the forward roll illustrated in Figure 68. Here your arms and feet strike the mat as your body rolls forward in a motion like that of a somersault. Be sure that the hand which serves as a fulcrum is placed on the mat turned in at an angle of about 45 degrees so that you can roll over the bent elbow in such a way as to prevent injury.

In the technique illustrated in Figure 69 you advance your right foot forward a little, then put your right hand on the mat turned in. Push the mat with your left leg, and your body will roll forward, completing a forward somersault. Your right elbow, shoulder, trunk, right side of the waist, outside of the left leg and foot, and sole of the right foot touch the mat in this consecutive order.

Next, try the variations illustrated in Figure 70.

67. Basic exercise in using feet
and arms to break a fall.

68. Forward roll: start and finish.

69. Technique of right forward roll.

70. Practice in jumping over an obstacle.

Explanation of Throwing Techniques

1. *Uki-goshi* (hip throw)

Momentum can be classified into two types. One is the force that acts along a curved line; the other is a force that acts along a straight line. The technique that best illustrates the former is *uki-goshi* (hip throw), while the one that shows the latter to best advantage is *uki-otoshi* (floating drop). Let us study *uki-goshi* first, since it demonstrates most effectively how to produce the largest curved-line momentum possible when you pivot against your opponent and at the same time induce momentum in him.

You and your opponent hold each other in right natural posture. Without making him bend his waist or his knees, you force him to lean toward his right front corner. Losing no time, you pivot to the left, putting your right foot inside his right foot and your left foot inside his left foot. Then put your loins and the right part of your back in close contact with his chest and abdomen by pulling his right sleeve with your left hand and pressing his back from the right side with your right hand and arm. Twist your loins from right to left, availing yourself of the strength with which you turn to the left. He will then be thrown as Figure 71 shows.

DYNAMIC EXPLANATION: When you turn to the left, the momentum mv is produced. This momentum is induced in your opponent with both your hands. Take the force produced by this as F. When the force F acts on his upper body, the small of your back, O, serves as a fulcrum. Therefore your opponent is thrown down, rotating around your loins by the moment FL, as shown in Figure 71.

KEY POINTS:

a. When you apply this technique, you must twist your loins without lifting them. You must make the maximum use of the momentum that works horizontally along a curved line.

b. When you pivot, you must keep your body upright. Do not bend either your waist or your knees. This enables you to twist your loins with greater speed. It also enables you to put both your loins and the right part of your back into close contact with your opponent's abdomen and chest in order to execute the throw correctly.

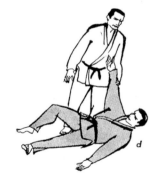

71. *Uki-goshi* (hip throw).

2. *Uki-otoshi* (floating drop)

This technique best illustrates the use of the waist and abdominal region to take advantage of momentum working along a straight line. In *uki-otoshi* you throw your opponent with momentum alone. You and your opponent hold each other in a right natural posture. As your opponent pushes you back, you withdraw more than he pushes. You break his posture to the front by taking advantage of his pushing force and the momentum produced when you withdraw. Suddenly you pull him down and forward with both hands, making use of the momentum produced when you drop your left knee to the mat. He is then thrown forward and down.

DYNAMIC EXPLANATION: As your opponent moves forward, the momentum mv works on his body. As you withdraw in the same direction, the momentum $m'v'$ works in the same direction on your body. Taking advantage of the combination of the two momentums, you break his posture to the front. Losing no time, you pull him down by the momentum produced when you suddenly drop your left knee to the mat. Since you pull down his upper body with both hands before he can step forward and regain his natural posture, his right toes serve as a fulcrum in the throw. He is thus thrown in a 270-degree arc.

KEY POINT: If you withdraw only as much as your opponent pushes, you cannot break his posture, nor can you pull him down by making his right toes serve as a fulcrum. Consequently, you must withdraw more than he pushes and at the same time put yourself in a position convenient to pull him down with the largest force and in the shortest time possible.

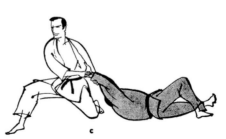

72. *Uki-otoshi* (floating drop).

3. *O-goshi* (major hip throw)

If you can support your opponent's center of gravity, you can easily rotate him around your waist by applying a small force on his upper body. It does not matter how much he weighs. *O-goshi* is typical of the techniques applied in this manner. Let us study the technique.

You and your opponent hold each other in a right self-defensive posture. Slipping your right hand beneath his left elbow, you put the palm on his back as deeply as possible. Lift his body gently with your right hand and arm while you pull him to the front by pulling his right sleeve with your left hand. Now, bending your knee a little, you advance your right foot inside his right foot so that it becomes parallel with it. Simultaneously you pivot your left foot near his left foot. Support his center of gravity from beneath with your back and waist, as shown in Figure 73. Twist your waist quickly from right to left. He will then be thrown, rotating around and over your hip.

DYNAMIC EXPLANATION: *O-GOSHI* looks a great deal like *uki-goshi,* but they differ considerably. In *uki-goshi* your hip serves as a fulcrum by being placed against your opponent's abdomen; in *o-goshi* it does so by supporting his center of gravity from underneath. Thus, in *uki-goshi,* you can make him rotate around your hip without any opposition from his gravity. But in *o-goshi* you must turn in against him with your hip lowered a little so as to support his center of gravity with your hip from underneath. In *uki-goshi,* on the other hand, you do not bend either your waist or your knees. Only *P* (see Figure 73) can be considered the force that throws him. This is the force with which you bend the upper part of your body to the left, twisting your waist from right to left with a quick spin, as if you were a spinning top.

KEY POINT: The key point of *o-goshi* is to pull the upper part of your opponent's body forward with your hands and completely support his center of gravity with the small of your back and your hip. Then throw him up and over the hip and down to the mat.

73. *O-goshi* (major hip throw).

4. *Tai-otoshi* (body drop)

In *tai-otoshi* you throw your opponent by making use of his own gravity and advancing force. You hold each other in natural posture. Making use of the force with which your opponent moves forward, you make him lean forward to his right front corner. Now you quickly turn to the left while pulling him down in his off-balance direction with both your hands, as shown in *b* and *c* of Figure 74. He will then be thrown in front of you, as shown in *d*.

DYNAMIC EXPLANATION: There is one force that you apply on your opponent. This is the force *F,* with which both your hands pull his upper body horizontally in the direction of the arrow. It is produced by the momentum *mv* arising from your turning to the left. Since *F* acts on his upper body, he falls forward (arm *L*) with his right foot serving as a fulcrum, as shown in Figure *74b, c,* and *d.* Since your right foot is thrown in front of his right foot, he cannot regain his balance by advancing his right foot.

KEY POINT: Your best chance to apply this technique is when your opponent has stiffened his body a little without bending his legs and is leaning forward or to his right front corner, as illustrated in Figure 74*a.*

74. *Tai-otoshi* (body drop).

5. *Tsurikomi-goshi* (lifting hip throw)

Look again at the discussion of moment of force in Chapter 6. You know that the larger the arm of the moment of force (Figure 54), the more efficiently you can use the force. Therefore, in attacking your opponent, you must apply force with the longest arm possible. *Tsurikomi-goshi* is typical of the techniques that make use of the moment of force.

It may be difficult for you to apply such hip throws as *harai-goshi* (sweeping loin) or *hane-goshi* (spring hip) on your opponent if he leans backward with his abdomen pushing forward. This, however, is a good chance for applying *tsurikomi-goshi*. With the principle of the moment of force in mind, let us study *tsurikomi-goshi*.

You and your opponent hold each other in a natural posture. You grasp the back part of his right collar with your right hand. The moment you break his posture to the front, you turn your body to the left while fully bending both your knees. You then put your lower back almost against his knees and your back against his abdomen, as shown in Figure 75b. You pull down his upper body with both hands while lifting his lower body backwards with your hips by pushing the mat with both your legs. He will then roll over your hip and down in front of you in the order of c and d in Figure 75.

DYNAMIC EXPLANATION: There are two forces that act on your opponent. The first is the force Q, with which you pull him down with both your hands. The second is P, with which your hip lifts his lower body up and backwards. Suppose that P is composed of the two forces P' and Q' and that Q' is equal and opposite to Q. Then the two forces Q and Q' work as a couple to rotate your opponent around your hip. The force P', which is the remainder, works to lift him. Therefore he is thrown down as shown in Figure 75c and d.

KEY POINT: If you turn to the left with your hip fully lowered, the arm L becomes longer, and the force P, which lifts your opponent's lower body backwards, becomes larger also. Therefore little effort is needed in performing this technique.

75. *Tsurikomi-goshi* (lifting hip throw).

6. *Harai-goshi* (sweeping loin throw)

Harai-goshi evolved from *uki-goshi*. In *harai-goslii* the problem of producing a momentum and inducing it in your opponent is the same as in *uki-goshi*, so when you pivot against him to apply force on him, you can do it in the same way as in *uki-goshi*.

You and your opponent hold each other in right natural posture. Then you take advantage of the force with which he pushes you back, and you cause him to lean to the front or to the right front corner. Now you quickly pivot to the left, drawing your left foot near to his left foot and bringing your right hip just in front of him while pressing his chest against your right side with your left hand. At the same time your right hand, which is placed under his armpit, pulls his back forward. Now you sweep up his lower body with your right leg and loin, bending your upper body to the left. He will then be thrown to the mat easily, as Figure 76 shows.

DYNAMIC EXPLANATION: There are three forces that act on your opponent. The first is the force F produced by the momentum mv, which arises from your pivoting to the left. The second is the force P, with which you bend your upper body to the left. The third is the force Q, with which you sweep his lower body upwards. Suppose that P and Q serve as a couple. They then set your opponent in rotation, with your right hip as a fulcrum. As for force F, which is very large, a moment is produced with your right loin as a fulcrum. Your opponent is then thrown to the mat.

KEY POINT: YOU must press your opponent's chest close to your right side with both your hands; otherwise, you cannot cause him to lean forward. If you fail to do this, his weight presses his feet against the mat, with the result that the friction created between the soles of his feet and the mat will prevent his body from being lifted from the mat.

76. *Harai-goshi* (sweeping loin throw).

7. *Hane-goshi* (spring hip throw)

Hane-goshi is very much like *harai-goshi* in form, but actually they are quite different. The latter evolved from *uki-goshi,* where the force works horizontally along a curved line, but the former might be considered a modified form of *o-goshi,* where your opponent's center of gravity is supported by your hip from underneath.

You and your opponent hold each other in right natural posture. Making him lean to the front or to the right front corner, you pivot to the left while lowering your right hip a little to support his center of gravity on it. At the same time you press the upper part of his body close to the right side of your body with both hands. You then lift him up with your right leg and hip and at the same time turn your upper body to the left. He will then be thrown, as illustrated in Figure 77*d.*

DYNAMIC EXPLANATION: There are four forces that act on your opponent. The first is the force F produced by the momentum *mv,* which is created by your pivoting quickly to the left. The second is the force *P,* with which you turn your upper body to the left. The two forces *P* and *F* combine into the larger force *R,* which rotates your opponent's body with your right hip as the fulcrum *O.* The third force is *Q*: the force with which your right leg lifts him up while your right hip serves as the fulcrum *O.* Suppose that the resultant *R* equals *P'* plus *Q'* and that *Q'* is equal and opposite to the force *Q.* Then *Q'* and *Q* work as a couple that turns your opponent about the fulcrum *O.* The remaining *P'* of the resultant *R* and the fourth force *P",* with which your left leg pushes the ground, produce a force that lifts him up and forward, as shown in Figure 77*d.*

KEY POINT: You should bring your opponent's center of gravity above your right hip by the force *F.* If you do not achieve this, friction will be produced between his feet and the mat, since his weight presses his feet against the mat when your right leg strikes against his, as in the case of *harai-goshi.*

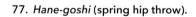

77. *Hane-goshi* (spring hip throw).

8. *Hiza-guruma* (knee wheel)

When you glide down a slope on skis, you bend both knees and lower your waist because this makes it much easier for you to control your balance. Consequently, if one knee cannot move freely, it will be difficult to balance yourself. The technique of *hiza-guruma* rests on this principle.

You and your opponent hold each other in right natural posture. You try to make him lean to the left front corner. The moment his weight rests on his left leg, which is bent a little at the knee, you put your left foot, with the toes turned in, to your left front corner near his right foot, as shown in Figure 78*b*, and break his posture to his left front corner. With your right hand, which holds his left sleeve, pull toward your right in a circular motion, at the same time putting the sole of your right foot on the outside of his left knee. Your left hand helps the pull of your right hand by lifting his right arm. His knee will then rotate around your foot, and he will fall to the mat.

DYNAMIC EXPLANATION: There are two forces that act on your opponent. The first is F, with which your hands pull his upper body in the direction shown by the arrow (Figure 78*b*). F is produced by the momentum mv, which arises from your pivoting to the right. The second is P', with which you prevent him from advancing his left foot. Suppose that F is equal to P plus Q and that P is equal and opposite to P'. Then P and P' will work as a couple to make your opponent rotate about his center of gravity. Since your right foot prevents his left leg from advancing, his left foot serves as the fulcrum O. As the remaining Q of F works on his upper body, QL, the moment of Q, will be produced about the fulcrum O to make him fall forward. He will then be thrown in the order shown in Figure 78.

KEY POINTS:

a. Pivot to the right with your left toes turned inside in order to make the rotating motion easier.

b. Refer to Figure 78*b* for the direction in which to pull your opponent's sleeve.

c. When you put your right foot on your opponent's left knee, you press the outside of his knee inward with your right big toe to rob him of the force of the left knee.

78. *Hiza-guruma* (knee wheel).

9. *Harai-tsurikomi-ashi* (lifting foot sweep)

When both knees are bent, they serve to change and control the balance of the body. Therefore, for instance, when your opponent leans forward toward the left, you attack his left knee with your right foot. But when he stands without bending his knees, it would be useless to attack the left knee. In such a case you should attack his left ankle instead of his knee, since the arm of the moment of force becomes longer. If you understand this rule, you will be able to understand *harai-tsurikomi-ashi* very well.

You hold your opponent by his right and left sleeves. When he is about to lean to his left front corner, you pull strongly with your right hand in the direction of your right back corner and push him to his left front corner with your left hand while letting your body pivot to the right, as shown in Figure 79b. At the same time you sweep between his knee and the outer part of his ankle with the sole of your right foot. He will then be swept and thrown forward.

DYNAMIC EXPLANATION: There are two forces that act on your opponent. The first is the force F produced by the momentum mv, which arises from your pivoting and twisting your body to the right. The force F works as the force with which you pull him forward by using both your hands. The other is the force P, with which you sweep his left leg with your right foot. Suppose the force that pulls him is composed of the two forces P' and Q and that P' is equal and opposed to P. Then P and P' work as a couple to rotate your opponent. The remaining force Q makes him fall forward, with his left toe as the fulcrum O. He will then be thrown, making a 270-degree turn, as shown in Figure 79.

KEY POINTS:

a. You should pivot to the right with your left toes turned in to make your rotating motion easy.

b. Your left hand pushes your opponent's body up and forward so as to help the pull of your right hand.

79. *Harai-tsurikomi-ashi* (lifting foot sweep).

10. *De-ashi-harai* (advanced foot sweep)

Imagine walking on a frozen road in the winter. Stepping carelessly, you sometimes slip and fall on your back on the road. What causes this to happen? The reason is that there is little friction between your feet and the icy road. If you have noticed this, you will easily understand the principle of *de-ashi-harai*.

You and your opponent hold each other in right natural posture. When he advances inward with a larger step than usual (see Figure 80*b*) you place your right foot at the back of your left foot. The moment he rests almost half his weight on the advanced foot, you sweep the ball of your left foot against the heel of his advanced foot just below the tendon of Achilles, at the same time pulling him to his right front corner. He will then be thrown, as Figure 80*c* shows.

DYNAMIC EXPLANATION: There are three forces that act on your opponent. The first is the force P, with which you sweep away his advanced foot. The second is the force Q, with which you pull him down with your left hand. The third is the momentum mv, which is produced when he steps forward with his right foot. The force P overcomes the friction between his right foot and the mat and enables you to complete the sweep. Both the force Q and the momentum mv act together to make him fall the instant his foot has been swept away.

KEY POINTS:

a. You should apply this technique the moment your opponent has placed almost half his weight on his advanced foot and is just about to put his entire weight down. At this moment he cannot easily shift the direction of his advanced foot.

b. Therefore timing is very important in the execution of this technique.

c. When you sweep his advanced foot, you push his left shoulder with your right hand so as to make his upper body turn up.

a

P

b

c

80. *De-ashi-harai* (advanced foot sweep).

11. *Okuri-ashi-harai* (sweeping ankle throw)

Knowledge of the rolling motion of a rowboat will help you understand the nature of *okuri-ashi-harai*. If you try to upset the boat for fun, you must push its lower side so as to create the rolling motion. By doing this, you are making use of the law of the resultant. What we do in trying to upset a boat we may also do in throwing an opponent in judo.

You and your opponent hold each other in main natural posture. He advances to the left. Taking advantage of his motion, you push him in the same direction, as if to scoop him with both your hands and break his posture to the right. Remind yourself of the rolling of a boat. When he has drawn his right foot close to his left foot and lets almost half of his weight rest on it, you sweep the sole of your left foot against his right, just above the ankle. At the same time you pull down his right sleeve with your left hand. He will then be thrown because both his feet are swept away, as shown in Figure 81*c* and *d*.

DYNAMIC EXPLANATION: There are four forces that act on your opponent. The first is the force with which you lift his body with a scooping motion. The second is the force P, with which you sweep your left foot against his right one to overcome the friction between it and the mat. The third force is the gravity G. The fourth is the force Q with which you pull him down. The gravity G and the force Q act together to make him fall on the mat since both his feet have been swept away.

KEY POINTS:

a. A good chance to apply this technique is when your opponent draws his right foot close to his left foot and rests almost half his weight on it.

b. Your left leg should be extended as you sweep.

81. *Okuri-ashi-harai* (sweeping ankle throw).

12. *O-soto-gari* (major external reaping)

In *o-soto-gari* you must reap one of your opponent's legs when his weight rests upon it, just as a scythe cuts grass. Reap only after you have unbalanced him to his right or left back corner. If you apply your technique before this, the friction produced between his foot and the mat will resist your further reaping force. Let us study this technique.

You and your opponent hold each other in right natural posture. Stepping with your left foot to his right side, you unbalance him backwards so as to make his weight rest on his right heel. This makes it difficult for him to move his right leg. Now quickly strike the right side of your chest against his right chest. At the same time you reap his right leg with your right leg as shown in Figure 82c. He will then be thrown on his back, as Figure 82 shows.

DYNAMIC EXPLANATION: There are two forces that act on your opponent. The first is the force F produced by the momentum mv, which arises from your chest striking against his. The other is the force P, with which you reap his right leg with your right leg; that is, the calf of your right leg. In Figure 82 the two forces are equal and opposite in direction. Therefore they act on him as a couple and set him in rotation.

KEY POINTS:

a. You should reap your opponent's right leg quickly so that he cannot shift his weight from the right foot to the left.

b. Sweep with the calf of your leg.

c. Point the toes of the sweeping foot to create a stronger sweeping force.

82. *O-soto-gari* (major external reaping).

13. *O-uchi-gari* (major inner reaping)

If you stand with your legs spread wide apart, you cannot shift your weight from one leg to the other quickly. *O-uchi-gari* takes advantage of this weakness in an opponent.

You and your opponent hold each other in right natural posture. You pull him to his left front corner with both your hands. Since this causes him to take a larger step than usual to the left front, you break his posture to his left back corner by pushing against his left shoulder with your right hand. Losing no time, you strike your right chest against his left chest and push him backwards with your right hand while reaping his left leg with your right leg in a circular motion from the inside, as shown in Figure 83c. He will then be thrown on his back, as Figure 83 illustrates.

DYNAMIC EXPLANATION: There are three forces that act on your opponent. The first is the force F, with which you push his chest backwards with your right hand. F is produced by the momentum mv, which arises from your striking your chest against his. The second is P, with which you reap his left leg. The third is Q, with which you immobilize his right arm. Suppose that F is equal to P' plus Q' and that P' is equal and opposite in direction to P. Then P' and P work as a couple to make your opponent rotate about his center of gravity. Since the remaining Q' of F acts on his upper body to make him fall backward, his right heel serves as the fulcrum O. Therefore the moment $Q'L$ about the fulcrum O works to make him fall backward, and he will be thrown on his back, as shown in Figure 83d.

KEY POINTS:

a. You must reap your opponent's left leg smoothly, just when he rests almost half his weight on it, so as not to create frictional resistance between his foot and the mat.

b. If he shifts his weight from the left foot to the right, your reaping action will be ineffective. Therefore you must push him with your right hand toward his left back corner to prevent him from putting his weight on his right leg.

83. *O-uchi-gari* (major inner reaping).

14. *Ko-uchi-gari* (minor inner reaping)

If you stand with both your feet wide apart, you will have difficulty shifting your weight from one leg to the other quickly, as we observed in discussing *o-uchi-gari* above (Figure 83). If you stand with both your knees bent a little, your waist lowered, and your feet wide apart, the same condition will exist. If your opponent stands in such a bad posture, it becomes easier for you to throw him down, since his center of gravity is lower than yours, and his position prevents him from changing his stance quickly. *Ko-uchi-gari* is the technique that takes advantage of this condition.

You and your opponent hold each other in right natural posture. When he spreads his legs more widely than usual and lowers his waist a little, you unbalance him to his right back corner by pushing with your right hand while pulling with your left hand, as shown in Figure 84*b*. At the same time you push him backwards with your right hand by taking advantage of the force with which you strike the right part of your chest against his. You pull his right sleeve downward with your left hand while reaping his right heel from the inside with your right foot. He will then be thrown on the mat, as shown in Figure 84.

DYNAMIC EXPLANATION: There are four forces that act on your opponent. The first is the force *P*, with which you reap his foot. If you reap his right foot, he is forced insufficiently to support his body weight on one leg only. The second is the force *Q*, with which you pull his right sleeve downwards with your left hand. The third is the gravity *G*, which acts on him vertically. The force *Q*, with which you pull downwards, and the gravity *G* result in a larger force that also pulls him downwards. The fourth force is *F*, which is produced by the momentum *mv* created when you advance your body against his. Force *F* acts on him to push him down and back. When he is thrown backwards, the heel of his left foot works as a fulcrum, as shown in Figure 84*b* and *c*.

KEY POINTS:

a. You should reap your opponent's leg as soon as you push his upper body, but never before. In fact, it is better to push before reaping.

b. You must push him back in the direction perpendicular to the straight line passing through both his heels; otherwise, he will shift his weight to his left foot.

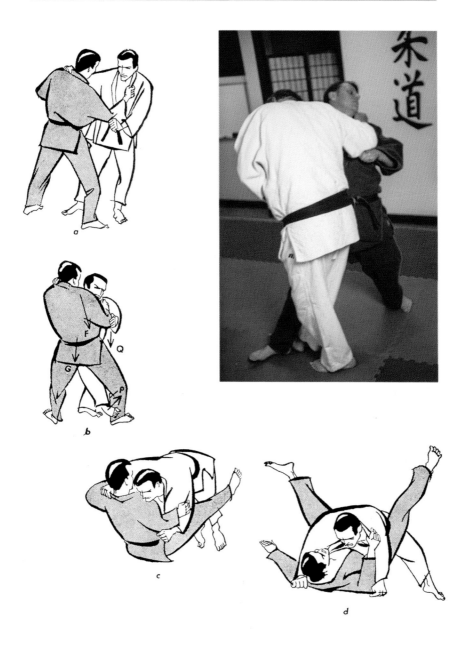

84. *Ko-uchi-gari* (major inner reaping).

15. *Tomoe-nage* (circle throw)

We sometimes see a boy clinging to his father's shoulders with his hands. As a result, the father staggers forward. What causes this to happen? The reason is that a new center of gravity is created between the father and the boy and that its position is outside the base of the father's balance. If the boy throws himself backward and at the same time pushes up the lower part of his father's abdomen from underneath with his foot, what will happen? A clear understanding of what happens in this case will help you to understand why a large man can be thrown by a small man. Let us study the technique of *tomoe-nage.*

You and your opponent hold each other in right natural posture. Availing yourself of the force with which he pushes you backwards, making his left foot advance, you unbalance him forward. You quickly slide your left foot as far as possible between his feet and simultaneously place the sole of your right foot against the lower part of his abdomen. If you bring your right knee in contact with your own chest, the placement of your right foot against his abdomen will be naturally correct. Falling on your back, you pull his upper body downward with both your hands while springing up his lower body with your right foot. He will then be thrown over your head in a circular movement.

DYNAMIC EXPLANATION: There are two forces that act on your opponent. The first is the force F, with which you pull his upper body with both your hands. Force F is produced by the momentum mv that is created by throwing yourself downwards to the mat. The second force is P, with which you push up his lower body with your right foot. Since the two forces P and F act on him together, they carry him over your head, as shown in Figure 85c and *d.*

KEY POINTS:

a. Slide your left foot between your opponent's feet as deeply as possible.

b. Drop your hip as close as possible to your left foot. This will produce a center of gravity between you and your opponent that will enable you to rotate him with ease.

c. Bend the knee of your throwing leg and touch your own chest with it before you execute the throw.

85. *Tomoe-nage* (circle throw).

16. *Uki-waza* (floating throw)

In *uki-waza* you apply with both your hands the momentum produced when you throw your body down to the side. There is a similarity between this technique and *uki-otoshi* (Figure 72).

You and your opponent hold each other in right defending posture. First you pull him to his left front corner. Next, you sway him to his right front corner. When he advances to the right front corner to retain his balance, you unbalance him by using his advancing force. Plant your right foot on the mat and slide your left foot outside his right foot, dropping the left side of your body on the mat. Then pull the upper part of his body with both your hands toward your left back corner by making good use of the force with which your body falls to the mat. He will then be thrown in the order of movements shown in Figure 86c and d.

DYNAMIC EXPLANATION: The force that acts on your opponent is the force F produced by the momentum mv that is created when your body drops to the mat, as shown in Figure 86c and d. The force F creates a moment, and his advanced right foot is the fulcrum. The force acts on him before he has time to escape by stepping over your extended left leg, and thus he is thrown.

KEY POINTS:

a. Since it may be difficult for you to throw your opponent in a full somersault with only the momentum mv, you must also take advantage of his advancing force.

b. To apply momentum on him with your hands, you must drop your left shoulder on the mat so that you can support your body at three points—your left shoulder and both your feet—in order to correctly execute the throw.

86. *Uki-waza* (floating throw).

8

How to Practice Grappling

Classification of Grappling Techniques

The term grappling is often inaccurately called *ne-waza*, which refers only to techniques of grappling performed in a sitting or lying position. The correct word is *katame-ivaza*, which refers to the execution of grappling techniques in a standing position (that is, locks and strangles) as well as in a lying position. Grappling is classified into three forms: *osaekomi-waza* (hold downs), *shime-waza* (strangles), and *kansetsu-waza* (elbow locks and twists).

1. *Osaekomi-waza* (hold downs)

These are techniques that are used to immobilize your opponent when he is lying on his back on the mat. They include *kesa-gatame* (collar hold), *kata-gatame* (single shoulder hold down), *kami-shiho-gatame* (four-quarter hold down), *kuzure-kami-shiho-gatame* (modified four-quarter hold down), and *yoko-shiho-gatame* (side four-quarter hold down).

87. *Kesa-gatame* (collar hold).

88. *Okuri-eri-jime* (sliding collar strangle).

2. *Shime-waza* (strangles)

These are techniques by which you strangle your opponent into submission. Both hands press against either the windpipe or the carotid arteries to stop the flow of blood to his head. If you do this, he will be forced to submit because of the lack of blood supply or else fall into unconsciousness. *Shime-waza* include such techniques as *nami-juji-jime* (normal cross strangle), *gyaku-juji-jime* (reverse cross strangle), *kata-juji-jime* (half cross strangle), *okuri-eri-jime* (sliding collar strangle), *kata-ha-jime* (single wing strangle), *hada-ka-jime* (bare-hand strangle), and *ryote-jime* (two-hand strangle).

3. *Kansetsu-waza* (elbow locks and twists)

These are techniques by which you bend, twist, or lock the elbow joint of your opponent's arm in order to bring him to submission. *Kansetsu-waza* include *juji-gatame* (cross armlock), *hiza-gatame* (knee-elbow lock), *ude-gatame* (straight armlock), and *ude-garami* (entangled armlock). Besides mentioning these pressure holds on the elbow joints, we may point out that even though locks on the other joints, such as the ankles or wrists, are effective, they are not allowed in the sport of judo.

89. *Juji-qatame* (cross armlock).

Because of the obvious danger if the other joints are involved, the rules of the Kodokan prohibit the locking of any joint except the elbow.

The Relation Between Grappling and Throwing

Suppose you are proficient in *o-soto-gari* (major external reaping—Figure 82) and not in other techniques. Look again at *de-ashi-harai* (advanced foot sweep) in Figure 80. Your opponent sometimes steps forward a greater distance than usual. That is your best opportunity to apply *de-ashi-harai*. Nevertheless, you may lose your opportunity because you are not a master of this technique. To take advantage of as many chances for attack as possible, you should, of course, master as many techniques as possible. The same thing can be said about the relation between throwing and grappling techniques: you must be proficient in both.

If you master both grappling and throwing, you will be confident enough during a tournament to proceed into grappling after you have executed an incomplete throw. After an incomplete throw, your opponent lies unbalanced on the mat. You are now conveniently set for attacking him by grappling. Without delay, you must seize this opportunity, which will enable you to win with little effort. Therefore both

90. First method of inducing momentum in a hold down.

throwing and grappling techniques must be used in a contest. In the next section let us consider how to attack in grappling.

Attack Methods in Grappling

Look at Figure 25 in Chapter 3. In grappling, the fundamental posture is a modification of the natural posture, which is the fundamental posture in throwing techniques. When you attack in accordance with the principle of this posture, you can produce the largest momentum possible and apply it at will. This is the basic reason for the discussion that follows.

1. Force must precede speed and lightness of motion in grappling

Generally, in grappling, force must precede speed and lightness of motion more than in throwing. In throwing, as in boxing, quick and large motions can be made freely, since the competitors face each other in a standing posture. In grappling, however, motions are restricted, since the competitors are close together in a lying position on the mat. Therefore you must attack your opponent with as large a force as pos-

91. Second method of inducing momentum in a hold down.

sible, at the same time making as much use as you can of quick and light movements.

Among the forces used, the most important is momentum. Look at Figure 92. You are advancing against your opponent as he lies on his back. You press against his chest region with your chest by grasping his trousers at the knees with your hands. What keeps your opponent down is the momentum produced when you press your body forward by pushing the mat with your legs.

Now look at *yoko-shiho-gatame* in Figure 109. By shifting your chest to the right, you press against your opponent's lower extremities with the right part of your chest as he tries to resist you by pushing up. When you shift your chest to the left, you press his chest down with the left part of your chest by means of the momentum produced when you shift your upper body sideways.

2. First consider how to produce the largest momentum possible and how to apply it effectively

From the above illustrations you will note that two methods enable you to produce the largest momentum possible and induce it most effectively in your opponent. One of these methods is to shift your body forward; the other is to shift your chest sideways. There are actually five ways of producing momentum, as we shall see later.

Look at Figure 90. Suppose you wish to exert as large a force as possible on your opponent's chest with your chest. You then let your body fall forward with your legs spread wide apart and your hands placed on the mat, the distance between them being equal to that between your shoulders, as shown in Figure 90a. Then push off the mat with your feet, keeping your elbows bent. Next lift your body so as to take the posture shown in Figure 90b. By this movement you can exert a large force, produced by the momentum mv on your opponent. You will notice that in this movement the point M of your chest describes the arc MM', while the gravity G that acts on you and the force P, with which you push the mat backwards, combine into the resultant R, as shown in Figure 90a. Thus you can push the ground backwards and bend your elbows so that the point M will pass the point N on the line of action of the force R. In actual contest, N is the point against which you direct your attack. You can induce in your opponent the momentum produced when you move your body forward. Then the m of mv represents the weight of your whole body.

Now look at Figure 91. Let us study a second way to produce the momentum mv and induce it in your opponent. Suppose you want to exert a large force on the point N' in the left front of your center of gravity. You then let your body fall forward with your right knee and right forearm on the mat. Rest almost the whole weight of your body on these points and make the big toe of your right foot stand on end. Push the mat with your right foot and right forearm while bending your left elbow. Just before your chest touches the floor, lift it so as to take the posture shown in Figure 91b.

In this motion, as in the one described above, the point M' of your chest will draw the arc $M'M''$, and the gravity that acts on your upper body will combine with the force P', which displaces your upper body toward the left front, to form the force R', which produces the momentum $m'v'$. Let the point M' pass the point N' on the line of action of the force R', and take the point N' as the area against which you will direct

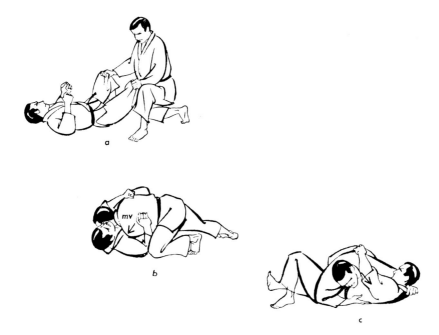

92. First method of immobilizing opponent by inducing momentum.

your attack in an actual contest. Then the momentum $m'v'$ will be induced in your opponent's chest. In this case, however, m' does not represent the weight of your whole body but only that of your upper body.

In both of the foregoing cases, as soon as the motions are over, return to the postures shown in Figures 90a and 91a, respectively. Repeat these exercises daily so that your arms will grow strong and your motions become faster. In exercising, you can save your energy if you use a ball to represent your opponent, as shown in the lower half of Figures 90 and 91.

3. Immobilize the force of your opponent's lower extremities

A man can walk and run easily when supported by his lower extremities, which he naturally takes for granted. In fact, the supporting force of the lower extremities is very great, as can be seen in their ability to kick or to push an object. It is plain that if your opponent makes use of

a   b

93. Second method of immobilizing
opponent by inducing momentum.

94. Third method of
immobilizing opponent
by inducing momentum.

a   b

his lower extremities to defend himself from your attack, he will be able
to push you off easily when you press your chest against his. Therefore
you should naturally try to prevent the use of the defending force of his
lower extremities. This is necessary in order for you to make free use of
the momentum that is produced when you press your body against his.
Let us study the methods of immobilizing the force of your opponent's
lower extremities.

In Figure 92 your opponent is lying on his back. In the fundamental
grappling posture, you grasp his trousers at the knees. Drop your hips
forward as quickly as possible by making use of the force with which you
are pulling his knees to your right back corner and of the force of your
kicking the mat backward with your right leg. You can then displace your
hips quickly to the front. This motion produces a large momentum. Try
to induce it in your opponent's chest with your chest by taking the position shown in Figure 92b. The force applied to him is so large that his
arms become too weak to oppose it. Now grasp his back collar with your
left hand while putting the strongest possible pressure on his chest. Then
hold his waist under your right arm. By taking this posture, you can apply
yoko-shiho-gatame (side four-quarter hold down—Figure 109).

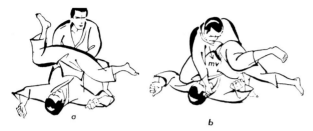

95. Fourth method of immobilizing opponent by inducing momentum.

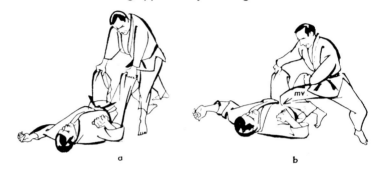

96. Fifth method of immobilizing opponent by inducing momentum.

Figure 93 demonstrates a second way of immobilizing the force of your opponent's lower extremities. You bring his left leg up to your right shoulder and by sliding your body to the same right side, you produce the momentum *mv*, as you do in carrying out the technique shown in Figure 92.

Figure 94 illustrates the way to make your body advance to the left side of your opponent while keeping pressure on his left leg. You bend his body in the shape of a lobster by carrying his left leg against your right shoulder, as shown in Figure 94*a*. Next you suddenly push his immobilized leg against his chest. The momentum will then be produced by this motion. Your opponent cannot push his leg back toward your chest because it is in close contact with his own chest. Completing the posture as shown in Figure 94*b*, you allow his leg to slide to the left. Then hold him on the mat with *yoko-shiho-gatame*.

A fourth method of immobilizing your opponent's lower extremities is illustrated in Figure 95. Your opponent's body, as in Figure 94*a*, is bent in the form of a lobster under the pressure of the lower part of your abdomen. He cannot use the force of his lower extremities or his waist and abdominal region. You advance your body by taking advantage of his immobilized condition. When you advance from the posture shown in Figure 95*a* to that shown in Figure 95*b*, the momentum *mv* is produced. Although it is not large, this momentum is induced in your opponent.

The fifth method of immobilization, shown in Figure 96, differs from the other four. Move quickly and advance your body, avoiding the resistance of your opponent's lower extremities. Grasp his trousers at the knees, as shown in Figure 96*a*. Then, as Figure 96*b* illustrates, you advance your body to the right side by putting your right knee on the right side of his abdomen and continue into the hold down.

Defense Methods in Grappling

Suppose you are placed in a disadvantageous position like the one shown in Figure 97. How can you then defend yourself from your opponent's attack? Since a large force is necessary in grappling, you must first regain your balance in order to make use of the force of your lower extremities. Then you can use the force of the waist and abdominal region most effectively and make all parts of your body cooperate as one force against your opponent's attack. You must be careful in both offense and defense to keep the source of power in your waist and abdominal region, which produces both momentum and muscular force. The movements of this region are activated by the help of the lower extremities.

Look at Figures 98 and 99. In Figure 98 your opponent (B) can neither strangle you (A) by the neck nor hold you down on your back, because you hold him between your legs. On the other hand, you can use both legs to push him back, rise up, or turn over to either side by making use of the force of the waist and abdominal region.

In Figure 99 you (A) put your left foot against the lower part of your opponent's abdomen while pulling him forward by the sleeve and lapel. He cannot move freely to the right or left. On the other hand, you can attack him by pushing him down on his back or making him roll forward. The key to defense in grappling is to keep your posture so as to be able to use at least one leg whenever it is needed.

97. Disadvantageous position in uncompleted throw.

98. Strangle
defense (1).

99. Strangle
defense (2).

100. Strangle
defense (3).

101. Disadvantageous position for defense.

Let us make the experiment demonstrated in Figure 100. Put both your hands and knees on the mat in order to take the posture of A in Figure 100. In this posture you can use the waist and abdominal region at will to defend yourself from an attack from the rear. Now have someone straddle your back and attempt a strangle from the rear, as shown in Figure 100. He probably cannot succeed as long as you hold this posture, since all your muscles will cooperate to defend you from the back strangle. The force of the waist and abdominal region, which enables all your muscles to cooperate, comes from the power of your legs, which press against the mat. On the other hand, your opponent cannot use his whole force to choke you when he is in his present posture. Your defensive power is therefore larger than his offensive power. Never give him the opportunity to flatten your body against the mat, as shown in Figure 101, for in this posture you can use neither the force of your legs nor that of your waist and abdominal region.

The same thing can be said of all strangulation techniques. If only you are free to push the mat with one of your legs, it will be impossible for your opponent to strangle you. By pushing the mat effectively, you can set your body in a posture that will allow the power of the waist and abdominal region to operate in defense against the attack.

Explanation of *Oosaekomi-waza* (Hold Downs)

1. *Hon-kesa-gatame* (side collar hold)

This technique literally means to hold the opponent down in the form of a slanting scarf. It is typical of techniques that take advantage of the moment of force.

You turn your opponent on his back as shown in Figure 102*a*. You press his chest with the right side of your chest while you hold his right arm tightly under your left arm and his neck under your right armpit, as shown in Figure 102*b*. This method of holding your opponent down by making use of the law of reaction has already been discussed in Chapter 4.

DYNAMIC EXPLANATION: Your opponent must make all parts of his body work together to exert a stronger force to enable him to pull out his pinned arm. Therefore he must first pull the arm out from under your armpit and must next try to turn you over to the left with his left shoulder serving as a fulcrum. Two forces can be considered to act on him. The first is GL, the moment of the gravity G that acts on your center of gravity C. The second is the force P, with which you immobilize his arm when he tries to draw it out. With both of these forces acting on him, it is difficult for him to escape.

KEY POINTS:

a. You should not place your center of gravity too high on your opponent's chest.

102. *Hon-kesa-gatame* (side collar hold).

b. Without stiffening your body, be ready to exert a force on any part of his body whenever he may try to escape. (This is a key point in all grappling hold down techniques.)

c. Be alert to the motion with which he tries to draw out his pinned arm; otherwise, he will eventually achieve a force strong enough to turn you over.

2. *Kuzure-kesa-gatame* (modified side collar hold)

The difference between this technique and *hon-kesa-gatame* is that you do not hold your opponent's neck but slide your right hand under his left armpit and place it on the mat, as shown in Figure 103*a*. This form allows you to change your position easily. When it appears to be difficult for you to hold this posture, you must take advantage of its free mobility. Keep your body relaxed except at the waist and abdominal region, and use your right hand, which is placed flat on the mat, as a supporting force for your body in this hold down. It is impossible for your opponent to roll you over—for example, to your right side—because you are able to support your balance with your right hand.

DYNAMIC EXPLANATION: See *hon-kesa-gatame* above.

KEY POINTS:

a. The resisting force created by your supporting right hand on the mat is superior to any force created by your opponent in his attempt to roll you over his body.

b. Your entire body remains relaxed except that tremendous force must be placed in your abdominal region.

103. *Kuzure-kesa-gatame* (modified side collar hold).

3. *Kata-gatame* (single shoulder hold)

You turn your opponent on his back and hold him from the side by pinning both his neck and his right arm together between your right arm and neck, as shown in Figure 104*b*. Your right knee is pressed closely against his right hip. Consequently, he cannot roll his body either to the right or to the left to escape.

DYNAMIC EXPLANATION: There are two forces that act on your opponent. One is the force of your gravity that comes into action when he attempts to turn you over to the left with his left shoulder as the fulcrum *O*. To succeed in this, he must overcome the moment *LG* that is produced by this force of gravity. Since he is too weak to overcome this moment, he cannot roll you to the left. The second force acting on him is the force *P*, with which you lock his right arm and his neck together between your right arm and neck. If the force *P* is strong enough, he will not be able to make all parts of his body work together. Thus he will not be able to exert a strong enough force upon you to allow him to escape.

KEY POINTS:

a. Never release your hold, but keep your neck pressed strongly against his right upper arm. Otherwise you may allow him the chance to escape by rolling his body up to get free of your hold. (See Figure 104*c*.)

b. Put your right knee close to his right hip with the foot balanced on the big toe.

104. *Kata-gatame* (single shoulder hold).

4. *Kami-shiho-gatame* (four-quarter hold)

You turn your opponent on his back and press your chest against his, grasping his belt from both sides with your hands, as shown in Figure 105. Rest the weight of your upper body on his chest. You hold him down by taking the posture shown in Figure 105a. The forms pictured in Figure 105b and c may be considered as modified versions of this technique.

DYNAMIC EXPLANATION: There are two forces that act on your opponent. The first is the force F, with which both your chest and your arms put pressure against his when he moves to free his body. If he tries to get up from the right side by using his left shoulder O as a fulcrum, you push the right part of his chest with the right side of your chest and push the mat with your left foot. Thus he cannot succeed in his effort because a strong moment will be produced about the fulcrum O. This is the second of the two forces that act against him. When you shift your chest against his, momentum is produced to serve as you press. If you take the postures shown in Figure 105b and c, you can produce a larger momentum and get more stability.

KEY POINTS:

a. Without stiffening your body, be ready to exert a strong force with any part of it.

b. Always put strength in both your big toes for power.

105. *Kami-shiho-gatame* (four-quarter hold).

5. *Kami-shiho-gatame*: a slight modification

If your opponent is bigger than you, it may be difficult for you to continue holding him down with *kami-shiho-gatame* as it is described above. In this case a technique like the one shown in Figure 106 may be more effective for you. You turn your opponent on his back. Holding his right upper arm between your right upper arm and forearm, you grasp your own right lapel with your right hand, as illustrated in Figure 106*a* and, with your chest, press his upper arm against your forearm on the mat. Then with your left arm grasp the back of his collar, as illustrated in Figure 106*b*. Execute the hold-down by applying pressure with your chest against his, at the same time stabilizing your body balance by keeping your trunk parallel with his.

DYNAMIC EXPLANATION: This technique takes even more advantage of friction and moment than does the *kami-shiho-gatame* illustrated in Figure 105. The arm L is longer in Figure 106 than it is Figure 105. Suppose your opponent tries to make you turn over to the left by using his left shoulder O as a fulcrum. The moment he tries this, press his right upper arm down with your chest. A strong moment of force about the fulcrum O will be produced. Since he cannot overcome this moment of force, he cannot succeed in rolling you over. If he tries to pull out his locked arm while your chest presses it down against your wrist on the mat, friction will be produced to prevent him from escaping. Thus he cannot escape by rolling to the right.

KEY POINTS:

a. Keep your trunk always parallel with your opponent's, keeping his head on the left side of your abdomen.

b. The big toes of your feet stand on end for power and balance.

c. His upper arm must be pressed against the radius; that is, the thumb side of the forearm.

106. *Kami-shiho-gatame:* modified version.

6. *Kuzure-kami-shiho-gatame* (modified four-quarter hold)

The technique of *kuzure-kami-shiho-gatame* is one of the transformations of the *kami-shiho-gatame* illustrated in Figure 105. This hold down uses the moment more than it does momentum, as does the technique illustrated in Figure 106. It may be adequate to say that it is a transformation of *kesa-gatame* that allows you to make use chiefly of the moment of force by locking your opponent's arm under your armpit and thereby executing the hold down. Look at Figure 107. Sliding your right arm under your opponent's right upper arm and over it, you grasp the back part of his collar and hold his right arm tightly under your right armpit.

DYNAMIC EXPLANATION: There are two forces that hold your opponent down. The first is the force P, with which you hold him by the right arm under your right armpit. As for his defensive power, whether he can make all the parts of his body cooperate depends entirely on his right arm. Therefore he must first pull his right arm from under your armpit to regain its use. The second force that acts upon him is GL, the moment of the gravity G that acts on you. With his right arm he tries to make you turn over to the left, using his left shoulder O as a fulcrum. His right arm must conquer the resistance of your weight. Thus the distance between his left shoulder and the point that your weight rests on serves as the arm L of the moment. Since he cannot overcome this moment, he cannot make you turn over to the left and allow him to escape.

KEY POINTS:

a. Your opponent's right arm must be held firmly with your right hand and arm, which is placed on your right thigh, and pinned tightly under your right armpit.

b. Never place the center of your gravity on his chest, even if you push down his chest with yours.

107. *Kuzure-kami-shiho-gatame* (modified four-quarter hold).

7. *Kuzure-kami-shiho-gatame*: another modification

This technique has been devised to make the arm of moment longer than that of the other *kami-shiho-gatame* techniques as well as to make it easy for you to apply momentum to your opponent. You hold your opponent by the neck under your left arm, and your hands grasp the left side of his belt, as shown in Figure 108*b*. Spread your legs as wide as possible to make your posture stable, so that it will be easy to apply momentum. Make both your big toes stand on end. Then grasp the right side of his belt or trousers with your right hand and press down on his chest. With your chest, put pressure upon his chest tightly by pulling your left elbow.

DYNAMIC EXPLANATION: There are two forces that act on your opponent. The first is the force F, which is produced by the momentum generated when you push your chest against him as he tries to roll his body to either side by pushing up your chest with both his arms. Suppose he tries to make you turn over to the left by using his shoulder O as a fulcrum. Your gravity makes a moment about the fulcrum O, thus creating the second force. This is the moment GL, which is too strong for him to resist. Therefore he is unable to make you turn over to the left. If he uses his right arm in an effort to make you turn over, you must pin it to the mat with your abdominal force. (See Figure 108*c*.)

KEY POINTS:

a. Hold your opponent tightly by the neck under your left armpit by putting pressure on his chest with your chest.

b. Stand the big toes of both your feet on end for power and balance.

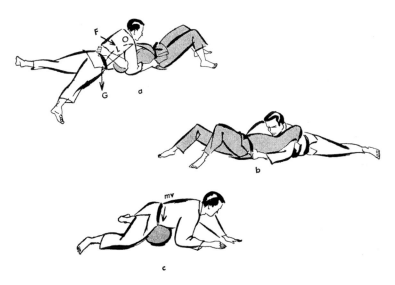

108. *Kuzure-kami-shiho-gatame*: another modification.

8. *Yoko-shiho-gatame* (side four-quarter hold)

You turn your opponent on his back and hold him down from the side in a right-angled position as shown in Figure 109*a*. You grasp his left lapel with your left hand after sliding it under his neck and around to the lapel. Then put pressure on his chest with your chest and grasp the back part of his trousers with your right hand after reaching between his legs. Extend your left leg with the big toe standing on end. Place your right knee close to the right side of your opponent's waist in order to deprive him of the force of his waist and abdominal region.

DYNAMIC EXPLANATION: There are two forces that act on your opponent. The first is the force F produced by the momentum with which your chest puts pressure on his arms and chest. Look at Figure 109*b*. In order to make all parts of his body work together, your opponent will try to roll to either side by pushing you up with both his hands and his left leg cooperating, as shown in the Figure. Nevertheless, he cannot succeed in this, once the force F works against them to press them down. If he tries to turn you over to the left by using his left shoulder as a fulcrum and pushing up your abdomen with his right hand, your gravity creates the moment GL about the fulcrum O to overcome his turning force. In this case, however, you should press your abdomen against his right arm on the mat. (See Figure 109*c*.)

KEY POINTS:

a. In order that your waist and abdominal region may function to the maximum, it is necessary that you stand both your big toes on end, thus stabilizing the balance and power of your body.

b. Press your right knee against your opponent's right side to prevent him from using the forces of his lower extremities.

c. Remember to press his right arm down with your abdomen whenever he tries to push you up with the arm.

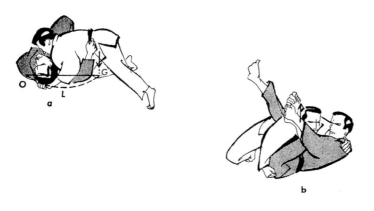

109. *Yoko-shiho-gatame* (side four-quarter hold).
Practice with rubber ball.

Explanation of *Shime-waza* (Strangles)

1. *Nami-juji-jime* (normal cross strangle)

As your opponent lies on his back, you straddle his abdomen in front and place both your knees on the mat. Grasp his left collar with your left hand and his right collar with your right hand in the regular hold as deeply as possible. (See Figure 110.) Strike your upper body towards his face, simultaneously pulling both your elbows outwards to create the proper pressure for the strangle.

DYNAMIC EXPLANATION: There are four forces that act on your opponent. The first is P, with which you pull your right hand to his left. Thus the little-finger edge of your right hand presses against his right carotid artery from the right side. The second is the force F produced by the momentum mv, which is created when you quickly press your upper body toward your opponent's face. This results in the creation of the moment FL about the fulcrum O with the effect that his neck is easily pressed from the left front side to complete the strangle. The other two forces are those duplicated on the left side of your opponent's neck. The combination of these forces results in the execution of the normal cross strangle.

KEY POINTS:

a. The movement of your arms must be a smooth movement parallel with the pressing forward of your chest against your opponent.

b. Your hands must be placed deep inside your opponent's collar.

c. When you apply *nami-juji-jime* from underneath, you must prevent your opponent from using the defensive power of his waist and abdominal region by breaking the posture of that region.

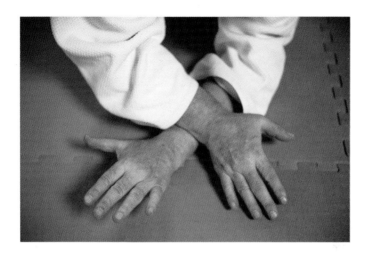

a

b

110. *Nami-juji-jime* (normal cross strangle).

2. *Kata-juji-jime* (half cross strangle)

If it is difficult for you to grasp both of your opponent's lapels as shown in Figure 110, then you may apply *kata-juji-jime* on him. Straddle him with one or both of your knees on the mat. Then grasp his left lapel as far back as possible with your right hand in the regular palm-down hold and with your left hand in the palm-up hold, as shown in Figure 111. Carry your right arm up and around his head toward your left and press the right side of his neck. (See Figure 111*b*.) Push down both your elbows while pulling them to the outside. Your right hand presses against his neck with its little-finger edge while your left hand presses with its thumb edge to execute the strangle. *Kata-juji-jime* can be applied from underneath too, as in *nami-juji-jime*. (Figure 110.)

DYNAMIC EXPLANATION: There are four forces that work on your opponent. The first is the force *P*, with which you pull your right hand to the left. Thus the little-finger edge of your right hand presses against his right carotid artery from the right side. The second force is *F*, which acts on your right elbow to push it down. This force is produced by the momentum *mv*, which is created when you make your upper body press forward toward your opponent's face. Therefore there is created about the fulcrum *O* the moment *FL*, which results in the pressing and strangling of his neck from the right front side. The third force, *P'*, is produced when the thumb-edge of your left hand presses his left carotid artery from the left side. The fourth is the force *F'*, which brings your left elbow downward to press against his windpipe from the left front side. *F'* is generated by the above-mentioned momentum *mv*.

KEY POINT: If you fall sideways while strangling your opponent, you must fall to the right side because your right hand is above the left; otherwise, your hold for the strangle will be broken.

a

b

c

111. *Kata-juji-jime* (half cross strangle).

3. *Kafa-juji-jime* (half cross strangle): a modification

Let us study a modification of *kata-juji-jime* in which we attack the opponent from the side. He is lying on his side on the mat, and you are standing by him on his left side. Lower your waist and place your left knee on the mat. You then grasp his left lapel as far around to the back as possible with your left hand, palm upward. With your right hand you grasp his right collar in the regular (palm down) hold. You then push him down with your right elbow while pulling your left hand to the left.

DYNAMIC EXPLANATION: See *kata-juji-jime* (Figure 111) above.

KEY POINT: In this technique your left hand cannot make use of the momentum that is produced when you press your body toward your opponent's face, since you sit at his left side. Therefore, in order to induce the whole of the momentum of your body into your right elbow, you should press your body toward your right elbow rather than toward your opponent's face.

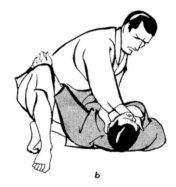

112. *Kata-juji-jime* (half cross strangle):
a modification.

4. *Okuri-eri-jime* (sliding collar strangle)

In both *nami-juji-jime* and *kata-juji-jime* you attack your opponent from the front. There are, however, some techniques in which you attack him from behind. Whenever he turns his back to you, you have a good opportunity to attack him. *Okuri-eri-jime* is one of the techniques of attack from the rear.

From behind, you grasp your opponent's left collar deeply with your right hand in the regular palm-down hold, placing your wrist under his chin. Grasp his right lapel with your left hand, which is inserted under and through his left armpit. (See Figure 113*b*.) Pull your right hand to the right and your left hand downwards to execute the strangle properly.

DYNAMIC EXPLANATION: There are two forces that you exert on your opponent's neck. The first is the force R, with which the thumb edge of your right hand presses against his left carotid artery from the left side toward the right or his windpipe from the front. The second is the force P, with which your left hand pulls his right lapel in a downward direction. When the force P acts on him, the reaction Q is produced. The two forces result in the force R', which presses against his right carotid artery from the right side. As the two forces R and R' press against his neck from three sides, the execution of the strangle is completed.

KEY POINTS:

a. You must first deprive your opponent of the force of his waist and abdominal region, as shown in Figure 113*c* and *d*, in order to immobilize the harmonious movement of all parts of his body.

b. With your right hand, grasp the farthest possible part of his left collar, and with your left hand, grasp his right front lapel. Pull his right lapel downward and his left collar toward the right side of his neck.

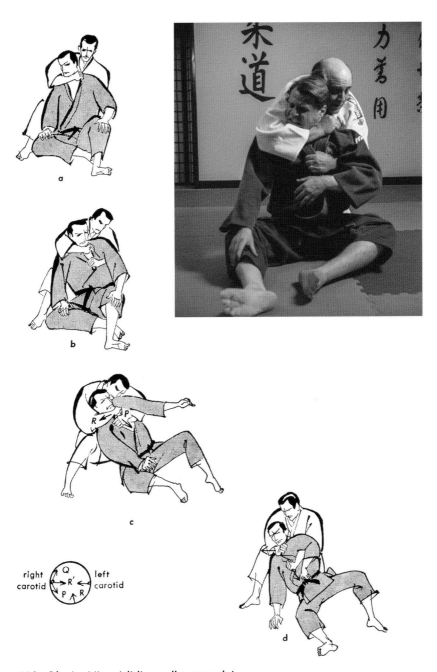

right carotid · left carotid

113. *Okuri-eri-jime* (sliding collar strangle).

5. *Yoko-okuri-eri-jime* (side sliding collar strangle)

Let us study a modification of *okuri-eri-jime* in which you attack the opponent from the side. Your opponent is on all fours on the mat as shown in Figure 114*a*. From his left side you grasp his right collar as deeply as possible with your left hand and press your left forearm against the right side of his neck. With your right hand, grasp his left lapel, as in *okuri-eri-jime*. Slide your right hip along the left side of his neck and shoulder, as shown in Figure 114*b*. Press your weight against his neck and pull him down forward to complete the strangle, using your right hand to draw down his left lapel while your left hand pulls and circles to the left side of his neck.

DYNAMIC EXPLANATION: There are three forces that act on your opponent. The first is the force F, which deprives him of the force of his waist and abdominal region. Force F is produced by the momentum mv, which is created when you pull him downward by taking advantage of your gravity. This force breaks his posture forward. The second force, P, is produced when you draw your left forearm from right to left. The third force, Q, is produced when your right hand pulls down on his left lapel. The combination of these three forces results in a completed strangle.

KEY POINTS:

a. You must grasp your opponent's right lapel first and place pressure on his neck before you attempt to reach across his right side and under it to grasp his left lapel. Otherwise, he is in a position to lock your right arm and roll you over to his right side for a counter-hold down like *kesa-gatame.*

b. When his posture is broken as he is pulled forward and down, he loses the use of the defensive power in his abdominal region.

114. *Yoko-okuri-eri-jime* (side sliding collar strangle).

6. *Kata-ha-jime* (single wing strangle)

Kata-ha-jime is another technique used in strangling an opponent from behind. The approach for this strangle is almost the same as in *okuri-eri-jime* in Figure 113. With your left hand, grasp your opponent's right collar deeply, using a regular palm-down hold and pressing your forearm against and under his chin. Slide your right forearm under his right arm and carry his arm up and over the nape of his neck (Figure 115*b*) while drawing your left hand from the right to the left side to strangle him into submission.

DYNAMIC EXPLANATION: There are three forces that act on your opponent. The first is the force *P*, with which your opponent's right collar presses against his own right carotid artery. The second is the force *Q*, with which the thumb edge of your left hand presses against both his windpipe and his left carotid artery from the front. The third is the force *R*, with which your opponent's own left shoulder presses the right side of his neck when his right arm is pulled around and behind his neck. The meeting of these three forces results in his being strangled.

KEY POINTS:

a. Keep your posture erect so that you can draw power from your waist and abdominal region.

b. Synchronize the movement of your right arm, which pushes his right arm up and backward, with that of your left hand, which moves horizontally from the right to the left.

c. Pull your opponent's body back in order to slant his upper body backward a little to the left. This will cause him to lose the resisting power of his waist and abdominal region.

115. *Kata-ha-jime* (single wing strangle).

7. *Hadaka-jime* (bare-hand strangle)

It has been mentioned that in the techniques of strangulation you press both your opponent's windpipe and the carotid arteries on either side of his neck. In *hadaka-jime* you place your left forearm against the right side of his neck and your left arm across the front of his neck. Your left palm is placed downward on the inner elbow fold of your right arm. Now bend your right arm backward and place your right palm against the back of your opponent's head. Your left arm rests on top of his left shoulder. In the technique of *hadaka-jime* you apply pressure with the left radius part of your wrist against the front of his neck. Then you push his head forward with the palm of your right hand while you draw your left forearm backward to complete the strangle.

DYNAMIC EXPLANATION: There are two forces that work on your opponent's neck The first is the force Q, with which your left forearm draws his neck backwards. The other is the force P, with which your right hand presses his head forward from the back. The synchronized operation of these two forces results in simultaneous pressure against the carotid arteries and the windpipe.

KEY POINTS:

a. Keep your posture erect.

b. Break your opponent's posture backwards (Figure 116*c*) to overcome his defensive power.

c. Your left forearm is drawn back—not pulled around—with the same pressure as that exerted by your right hand in pressing forward.

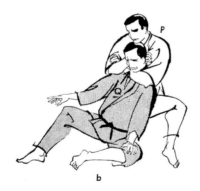

116. *Hadaka-jime* (bare-hand strangle).

8. *Ryote-jime* (two-hand strangle)

You grasp your opponent by both sides of his collar in the front with your hands in the regular hold (hands clenched, thumbs up), as shown in Figure 117. The little finger of your left hand is placed on his right carotid, and that of your right hand presses his left carotid. Now, with both your hands, press both sides of his neck at the same time, twisting your wrists inwards until the palms of both hands are turned upwards. The force applied to his neck is produced with the pressure of the front of your clenched fist or the lower part of your fingers. You can also strangle him from underneath.

DYNAMIC EXPLANATION: There are two forces that act on your opponent's neck. The first is the force P, which presses his windpipe and left carotid artery with your right little finger and the front of your fist. The other is the force Q, which presses his right carotid artery with your left little finger and the front of your fist. Since the two forces press both sides of his neck, both the supply of blood to his brain and his breath are stopped. The result is that your opponent is placed under complete submission by the strangle.

KEY POINTS:

a. Prevent your opponent's use of the defensive power of his abdominal region by pulling him down and forward, thereby breaking his posture. Complete the movement by pressing the weight of your hip region against the side of his neck. When you apply *ryote-jime* from underneath, you must break his waist posture by kicking his right thigh away with your foot.

b. Turn both your wrists simultaneously until pressure is created against both sides of his neck when the front of the fists of both your hands (palm up) twist into both sides of his neck to complete the strangle.

117. *Ryote-jime* (two-hand strangle).

Explanation of *Kansetsu-Waza* (Twists, Bends, or Locks Applied on the Elbow Joint Only)

1. *Hiza-gatame* (knee-elbow lock)

To produce a positive effect in locking, bending, or twisting your opponent's elbow joint, it is necessary to break his posture to prevent him from using the force of his waist and abdominal region before you apply the lock. Let us study the dynamic sphere of the elbow joint. Look again at the operation of the elbow joint as illustrated in Figure 35. When you lift a weight in your hand by bending the elbow joint, the head O of the radius (the bone on the same side of the forearm as the thumb) serves as a fulcrum. The head O' of the ulna (the bone on the same side of the forearm as the little finger), to which the biceps is attached, is the point of application. The hand G, which is carrying the weight, is the point of exertion. The lever arm of the pulling force P of the biceps is OO', and that of the weight is OG. Since OG is far longer than OO', the force P must be inversely larger than the weight in order to lift it. In locking, twisting, or bending the elbow joint of your opponent in judo, the resisting force of your opponent's arm is P, whose moment is POO'. Therefore you have an advantage over your opponent's moment POO' because you can easily apply a larger moment than POO' on the point G.

Now let us study the technique of *hiza-gatame*. You are lying on your back with the body of your opponent set between your legs. When he extends his right arm carelessly toward your chest, you quickly grasp the wrist tightly under your left armpit. At the same time you break his posture, as shown in Figure 118*b*, by pushing back his left thigh with your right foot while pulling his left lapel with your right hand. Now with your left knee press his right elbow joint from the outside while bending your body upward. He must give a signal for defeat because of the intense pressure on his elbow joint.

DYNAMIC EXPLANATION: You bend your body upward. Suppose the elbow joint O is the fulcrum. Then the moment of the force P, which lifts up the wrist, comes to be LP. On the other side, the resisting force R of the right elbow is not stronger than P, since P is the bending force of your upper body. Therefore you can create extreme pain in your

118. *Hiza-gatame* (knee-elbow lock).

opponent's right elbow joint. Also, if you press down on the elbow joint with your left knee, the result will be an even more unbearable pressure that will cause your opponent to submit quickly.

KEY POINTS:

a. Hold your opponent's right wrist firmly under your left armpit; otherwise, he may escape by pulling it away.

b. Push away at his left hip with your right foot in order to break his posture. He will then be unable to use the defensive power of his waist and abdominal region.

2. *Juji-gatame* (cross armlock)

This technique locks the opponent in the form of a cross. His upper arm is locked between your thighs, and pressure is applied upward against his elbow joint. As your opponent lies on his back, you sit at his right side, as shown in Figure 119*a*. When he carelessly extends his right arm toward your chest, you quickly grasp the arm and hold it in your arms. Now you turn your body to the right to sit at the right side of his right shoulder, as shown in Figure 119*b*. At the same time place your left leg over his neck and face to prevent him from rising. Your right leg is planted against his right side. While pinning his upper arm tightly between your thighs, you press it against your abdomen. Now pull his wrist with your hands so that the little-finger edge is pressed against your chest. At the same time raise your abdomen and place pressure against his elbow joint for the completion of the lock.

DYNAMIC EXPLANATION: Take your opponent's elbow joint as O and his hand as A. If you pull the hand toward you with the force P, then the moment of P about the fulcrum O will be produced. The moment PL can easily overcome the defensive power of your opponent's elbow joint.

KEY POINTS:

a. You must pull your opponent's right hand so that his little finger will touch your chest. Thus the inside of his arm is turned up.

b. Push your hips as close as possible to his shoulder for leverage support.

c. With the lower part of your left leg, pull his head against your hips to prevent him from raising his body.

d. Pin his upper arm by pressing your knees together.

e. Apply the final pressure by raising your abdomen.

119. *Juji-gatame* (cross armlock).

3. *Ude-garami* (entangled armlock)

In the above-described techniques you reverse the natural bend of your opponent's elbow joint. In *ude-garami,* however, you twist to apply pressure on your opponent. He lies on his back, and you sit at his right side. If he carelessly extends his right arm, you quickly grasp the wrist with your right hand, as shown in Figure 120*a*. Then you lean across his chest, bringing your left hand under his right arm and up to grasp your own right arm—left wrist on top. If you lift up his right elbow a little with your left forearm while pushing down his right wrist with your right hand, you will exert enough pressure on his elbow joint to bring about his submission.

DYNAMIC EXPLANATION: Your opponent's elbow joint can be taken as O and his wrist as A. When you push down on his wrist with the force P, the moment PL will easily overcome the resistance of his arm. Thus the extreme pressure placed on his elbow joint will cause him to submit to the lock.

KEY POINTS:

a. Lift your opponent's elbow and push down on his right wrist as he is lying on his back. The resulting moment PL will create a twisting of his elbow joint.

b. Apply the entangled elbow lock only when your opponent's arm is in a bent position.

c. Keep your body posture correct and lower your body in order to create a low center of gravity and thereby prevent your opponent from escaping.

120. *Ude-garami* (entangled armlock).

Index